THE ART OF SIMPLICITY

10 WAYS TO STREAMLINE YOUR LIFE AND FIND TRUE FULFILMENT

KC PALMER

For all booking enquiries including 1 on 1 or group sessions, speaking engagements, or media requests, please reach out to: consciousenquiry@gmail.com

Copyright © 2025 KC Palmer

ISBN: 978-1-7640764-0-1 eBook
ISBN: 978-1-7640764-7-0 Paperback

All rights reserved, including the right to reproduce this book or portions thereof in any form whatsoever. Apart from any fair dealing for the purpose of research, private study, criticism or review, no part of this publication may be reproduced, stored in or introduced into a retrieval system, or transmitted in any form or by any means (electronic, mechanical, photocopying, recording or otherwise), without the prior written permission of the copyright owner.

This book is dedicated to my beautiful family for their eternal love and guidance, and to the universe for its sacred teachings silently gifted in the air.

CONTENTS

Chapter 1: 1
The Magnetic Nature of Humanity

Chapter 2 23
The Human Mind and Computer Operating Systems Theory

Chapter 3 47
The Highway of Life

Chapter 4 61
The Iceberg of True Connection

Chapter 5 75
The Moth and the Flame

Chapter 6 91
Unravelling the Onion

Chapter 7 119
The Road to True Fulfillment

Chapter 8 139
Unplugging from the Machine

Chapter 9 157
The Dance Between Human Reflection and Reactivity

Chapter 10 175
Connect to Source and Integration

PROLOGUE

For as long as I can remember, I have been searching for something: a sense of belonging, a tribe, a purpose that truly resonated with the deepest parts of me. That search took me through the structured, disciplined world of the military—first joining at the ripe age of 17 in the Air Force, then into British Forces and, finally, a round in the Australian Army. Each step reinforced an identity built on resilience, discipline, and the pursuit of excellence. Yet, no matter how far I pushed myself physically or mentally, something always felt just out of reach.

The truth was, I had trapped myself in cycles of comfort disguised as challenge. The military gave me purpose, but also provided a structure where I didn't have to ask myself the more complex questions. It was a world where I knew my role, where hardship was expected and where my identity was defined by my rank, fitness, and ability to endure. But when the uniform came off, the real battle began. So I ran. Not away from anything, but towards the unknown.

In my twenties, I wandered through Europe and South America, driven by an insatiable curiosity and a hunger for something more profound. I stood in centuries-old cathedrals and walked through the ruins of fallen civilisations, feeling the weight of history pressing against my skin. I sat with shamans in the Amazon, drinking in their wisdom as I confronted the shadowed parts of myself I had long ignored. I met people who lived with so little but carried a richness of spirit I had never encountered in the structured worlds I had known.

Through these travels, I began to see patterns within myself and others and how we all seek meaning in our own ways. I recorded voice notes, scribbled thoughts on napkins and spent countless nights staring at the stars, replaying my past, dissecting my mistakes and searching for lessons hidden within them. A decade of this movement, stillness, and unlearning began forming something tangible.

The strategies I share in this book were not created in a moment of enlightenment, nor were they handed down by some wise teacher. They were forged in the fire of experience, failure, late-night realisations, pushing myself too far, and then learning how to come back. They are not just theories but lived truths born from my own journey of healing, growing, and simplifying the complex web of life into something that makes sense.

I am still on that journey. I am still learning. But what I have found and what I offer to you now is a way to see through the noise, to step outside the cycles we create for ourselves, to strip away what doesn't serve us and return to what does. This is not about achieving perfection but about embracing the *Art of Simplicity*—living with clarity, purpose, and an understanding that the answers we seek have always been within us.

INTRODUCTION

Welcome to the *Art of Simplicity*, a book I have carefully crafted with the simple but profound purpose of guiding you along this magnificent life journey. I have deliberately presented this book in a manner that does not reflect a step-by-step manual because life is not a process that follows a rigid, predictable pattern. Our Earth constantly shifts and changes, guided by seasons and natural events. When one is on the path of healing, learning and growing, it is not a set of instructions that enables such a transformation. In the same way, a caterpillar does not read the owner's manual before stepping into its cocoon. Life is a fluid stream of experiences, challenges and opportunities. Thus, the content within these pages is not intended to impose a methodical approach but to offer theories and tools in a flexible, adaptable form.

As you dive into the layers of these pages, you will encounter ideas meant to be absorbed in a way that suits your unique journey. I humbly acknowledge this book serves two purposes: to guide you and to fulfill my life's purpose of serving and sharing the knowledge I have gathered. If you walk away with even a single tool or method you can apply to your life by the end of this book, my goal to serve you has been accomplished.

These concepts are the silent whispers you hear on the gentle evening breeze. Once learned, they are placed in your mind like an array of mental tools, available when needed and ready to help you navigate whatever life brings. Some may require the utmost discipline with immediate action, while others may remain dormant like a crocodile in the water, silently waiting for the right moment to be called upon—deliberate and strategic.

Some elements are expressed technologically, designed to resonate with both older and newer generations. We live in a time where technology connects us all, and while not everyone will be drawn to every idea, I hope this book speaks to many, regardless of age or background. You will see practical tasks at the end of each chapter to reinforce the tools you have learnt and affirmation to plant the seeds in your mind.

Although this book is written objectively, you will discover a deeply personal showering of poems and quotes I have made along my journey. Life is a never-ending journey of lessons and teachings. In this book, I have carefully crafted and simplified 10 philosophies.

However, they were forged in the great depths of 10,000 mistakes. May these pages offer clarity, inspiration, and tools to embrace life's unpredictable flow confidently and gracefully.

Before we delve further, I urge you to engage in a vital exercise that will significantly enhance your understanding by the end of this book. Below are three timelines: Career, Relationships and Family. I encourage you to fill in your life's significant chapters and events. Use a pencil and add a dash on the line to create a new event on that timeline. This exercise is a crucial step in your journey of self-reflection and will be revisited in later chapters.

Family: Trauma, deaths, positives, negatives

Relationships: Lovers, friends, breakups, conflict

Career: Job starts, departures, promotions, struggles, conflict

---

Peace in Surrender

Crawling slowly, the caterpillar begins,
The transformation journey that happens within,
Green leaves and grey nights,
He continues to crawl with all his might,
But the pain does not slow him down,
For tomorrow, the future is neither lost nor found,
He enters his cocoon, one last glance at the sacred light,
The lonely space as dark as night,
He does not fear the holy womb,
The death of old, the eternal tomb,
Two weeks pass in isolation,
But he does not fret, only inward contemplation,
Only the present moment he knows is true,
He hatches from his cocoon, his wings electric blue,
Agile and vibrant, he flies around,
For tomorrow's journey is neither lost nor found.

-KC Palmer

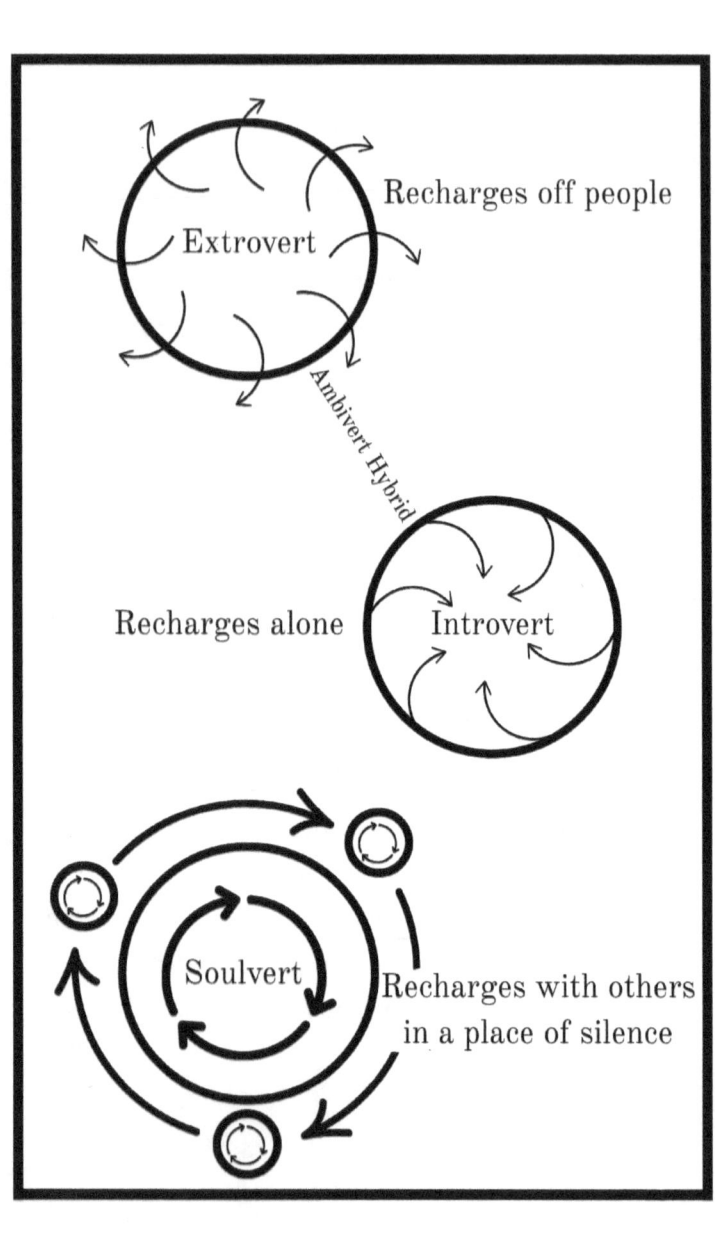

CHAPTER 1
THE MAGNETIC NATURE OF HUMANITY

"Even if you gained access to the entire universe's knowledge, what would you do with it, and who would you trust?" – KC Palmer

HUMANS, IN MANY ways, are like magnets. We carry an invisible energy, a magnetic charge that attracts or repels others, depending on the forces we emit. Just as magnets have positive and negative poles, we have energies that attract people to us or repel them. Our energy fields, thoughts, emotions, intentions, and actions work like a magnet's charge, creating an invisible aura that influences our world. The types of energy or charge we project are crucial for our well-being and play a significant role in shaping the people who enter our lives, including friends, partners, and lovers.

The Types of Charges: Positive, Negative, and Neutral

Like magnets, we all possess different types of charges. Some people exude positivity, like the North Pole of a magnet, drawing others in with their warmth, optimism, and kindness. These individuals tend to attract people who are also positive or supportive, creating a dynamic where they naturally align with those who encourage growth and connection. Their energy can attract friendships based on mutual support, partnerships built on trust, shared values and even romantic relationships that are nurturing and uplifting.

On the opposite end are those who radiate negativity, like the South Pole. These individuals often find themselves surrounded by people who share similar negative or emotionally draining attitudes. They may repel those with a more positive outlook but attract people who need support or are in similarly tricky emotional states. This charge can create a cycle of conflict or emotional turmoil in relationships, as both partners feed off each other's negativity. These individuals may find themselves stuck in unhealthy relationships or toxic dynamics unless they consciously try to change their energy.

Then, some hover in a neutral state, like a magnet that is not actively charged. These individuals may not radiate intense positive or negative energy, but they can serve as a balance in their environments. They may drift away from those seeking stability or understanding and may find themselves in less intense but more peaceful relationships. Neutral individuals are often the calming influence in a group of friends or a relationship. While they may not seek attention or validation, they can offer quiet support and a sense of grounding.

The Concept of Charging: Energy In and Energy Out

The more energy you put into the world, the more your battery depletes. Positive people, constantly emitting love, care, and enthusiasm, may eventually feel exhausted until they recharge. Their energy is a gift to others, but like any magnet, it requires balance. Without proper self-care, even the most radiant person can begin to lose their charge, leaving them vulnerable to the opposing forces that seek to drain their vitality.

Conversely, the less you put into the world, the more you charge. This isn't about becoming withdrawn or indifferent, but understanding the importance of internal balance. Just as a magnet can be recharged by realigning its poles, humans can recharge by retreating into themselves, taking time for reflection, meditation, prayer, or solitude. When we withdraw from draining situations, we allow our energy to realign, gathering strength to re-engage with the world. This principle is key in relationships. In friendships, partnerships, and romantic connections, ensuring you are not constantly giving without recharging can help prevent resentment and burnout.

There are people whose presence feels like an energy vacuum, a drain on our emotional, mental, or physical resources. Why is this? These individuals often project energy that demands more than it gives. They may be overly reliant on others for validation, constantly requiring attention, or expressing negativity that consumes the vitality of those around them. This draining effect is akin to a magnet that takes, without giving, attracting energy from others without replenishing its charge. Over time, this imbalance can leave those around them feeling exhausted, as though they have lost a piece of themselves in the interaction.

In relationships with friends, partners, or lovers, these people often create an uneven dynamic where one person constantly gives energy while the other takes it without offering much in return. This creates an unsustainable situation where the giver may eventually feel emotionally depleted or resentful. It's essential to recognise when someone's energy is draining and understand that it's okay to set boundaries or step back to protect your own energy.

The Energy Chargers: Why Do Some People Revitalise Us?

Some serve as chargers for others. These people seem to amplify the energy of those around them, filling others with enthusiasm, hope and motivation. How do they do this? Much like magnets that strengthen one another when aligned, these individuals project an energy that resonates with others in a way that lifts them. They inspire, offer empathy, or show up with a sense of understanding and positivity that encourages others to feel empowered.

Chargers are not necessarily positive in the conventional sense, but they can connect deeply, offering revitalising energy. Their internal charge seems inexhaustible because they have learned to balance giving and receiving. By replenishing their energy through self-awareness and care, they can share their charge without depleting themselves.

Chargers tend to attract people who need support or understanding in relationships, but they also know how to maintain healthy boundaries. They bring energy and balance to help rejuvenate those around them. These individuals tend to be the ones who create healthy, vibrant relationships, whether as friends, partners, or lovers, because they contribute to the emotional well-being of others without losing themselves in the process.

From a philosophical standpoint, the human battery metaphor also introduces more profound questions about the nature of self-care, autonomy, and interdependence. If we are all batteries, how do we relate to others regarding energy exchange? Is exploiting someone else's energy possible, or is that an inevitable part of social engagement? Do we create structures that allow individuals to recharge as a society, or do we demand constant outward-facing energy from everyone?

Moreover, the cultural context in which we live often privileges extroverted behaviours. The modern world, emphasising social networking, connectivity, and outward productivity, frequently demands that individuals expend energy at a pace that does not always respect the need for solitude and quiet reflection. This can lead to burnout, as introverts and even ambiverts find themselves in environments that are not conducive to their natural energy flow. In these cases, the metaphor of the human battery becomes a critique of societal expectations that fail to honour the diversity of energy needs.

Ultimately, the key to understanding human nature as energetic beings is recognising that we are in constant flux. Like magnets, we all can change our charge. We can align ourselves with positive forces or fall prey to negativity, attracting the right or wrong types of energy based on how we manage our internal magnetism. In relationships, our magnetic charge will attract certain people while repelling others. The people we draw into our lives reflect the energy we put out. If we radiate positivity and self-love, we are more likely to attract those with similar values and energy. Conversely, if we are constantly caught in negativity or emotional turmoil, we may find ourselves attracting people who mirror those struggles.

Recognising this dynamic, we can take responsibility for the energy we emit, understanding that by shifting our internal charge, we can change the types of people we attract into our lives. Whether seeking new friends, a life partner, or simply more harmonious relationships, the energy we project plays a pivotal role in our connections. It is within our power to align our magnetism with the relationships and energy we want to experience. Through self-awareness and balance, we can create a life filled with people who uplift, inspire, and recharge us.

The Correlation Between Battery Dynamics and the Human Condition

Understanding the human personality through the battery metaphor reveals the inherent need to balance giving and receiving energy. Though introverts and extroverts have differing modes of energy exchange, they experience the same basic principles of energy flow: storage, depletion, and recharging. The key lies in understanding one's natural tendencies and learning to harmonise them with the demands of the external world.

Consider a hybrid system where a human, like a battery, can fluctuate between being externally charged and internally recharged. This is often seen in individuals who exhibit characteristics of both introversion and extraversion, a phenomenon referred to as ambiversion. These individuals can adapt to different environments, engaging in social activities when they are energised and retreating when they need to replenish their internal reserves.

In this context, the ideal condition for any human might not be extreme introversion or extraversion but a nuanced and adaptive approach to energy management. Just as a battery works most efficiently when used according to its designed parameters, so do humans perform at their best when they respect the natural flow of their energy. Recognising when to engage and withdraw ensures that we maintain the equilibrium necessary for mental, emotional and physical well-being.

Extraversion: The Battery That Charges Through External Interaction

Extraverts are often described as people who recharge through social interaction, adventure and external stimulation. Like a battery connected to a power source, they thrive on external stimuli, drawing energy from their surroundings and the people they engage with. The more they interact, the more they feel energised, animated, and empowered.

In this model, an extrovert's energy flows outward, feeding off conversations, social events, and activities that provide a sense of connection and validation. This dynamic mirrors the way a battery releases energy to power external devices. An extravert's energy is not primarily self-contained but is continually replenished and renewed through external interactions. When isolated or alone, they experience a depletion of energy, akin to a battery losing charge when not connected to a charging source.

However, this reliance on external stimuli has its limits. No matter how efficient, a battery will eventually run out of charge if it cannot access a reliable power source. Likewise, extroverts can sometimes experience burnout when their interactions, while initially energising, become overwhelming or shallow. The balance between seeking stimulation and recharging is delicate, as constant external engagement can lead to emotional exhaustion if not moderated.

Introversion: The Battery That Charges Within

In contrast, introverts are individuals who tend to charge internally. They do not draw their energy from external interactions but cultivate it through solitude, reflection, and contemplation. Imagine a battery that recharges through its internal energy flow rather than relying on an external power supply. Introverts are recharged by introspective activities such as spending time in nature, reading, and journaling. They can withdraw from social situations and, rather than feeling depleted, experience renewal and re-energisation.

Unlike extroverts, introverts do not lose energy in solitude; they gain it. However, just as a battery can be overcharged, introverts can become overly absorbed in their inner world. A complete disconnect from others, prolonged isolation, or intense introspection can lead to stagnation or a sense of emotional depletion. Though introverts thrive in solitude, the balance lies in knowing when to re-engage with the world and when to retreat and recharge.

The Emergence of the *Soulvert*: A New Dimension of Human Energy

In the vast landscape of human personality, the well-known dichotomy of introversion and extraversion has long dominated psychological thought. Introverts are often described as individuals who recharge in solitude, while the presence of others energises extroverts. However, as we delve deeper into the complex nature of human energy, I have come to recognise a third and new archetype, which I have named the *Soulvert*. This word is not found in any dictionary and can be replaced with another word if it does not resonate.

A soulvert is a person who, like an introvert, finds peace and rejuvenation in solitude. But, there is a subtle yet profound difference: they recharge by being around others in quiet, serene environments. Unlike traditional extroverts, who thrive on dynamic and stimulating social interaction, soulverts absorb energy from people's presence but in a calm, peaceful, and unobtrusive way. Essentially, they are introverts who charge off people, yet they do so in a tranquil and soothing context rather than a lively or energetic one.

This discovery prompts us to reconsider how we categorise human personalities and their energy sources. It suggests that the relationship between human energy and social interaction is not as simple as a binary between alone and with others. Instead, it is a spectrum with unique variations that require a more profound understanding and exploration.

The Quiet Power of the Soulvert

The soulvert's most distinctive feature is their ability to draw energy from others without needing loud conversations or bustling environments. Imagine an individual who feels an undercurrent of energy flowing through them while in the company of others, but in settings that promote stillness and tranquillity, such as a quiet café, a peaceful gathering, or a retreat with a small group of people. The solvent thrives on the shared energy of others, but it is a subtle, quiet connection.

In a crowded room or at a party, the soulvert might feel overwhelmed or depleted, much like an introvert would. However, when placed in a serene environment with others who are similarly calm and reflective, the soulvert experiences a unique form of replenishment. If the energy is shared quietly and harmoniously, the mere presence of others fuels the soulvert's inner vitality.

In this sense, they are neither introverts nor extroverts in the conventional sense. They are a fusion of both, absorbing the energy of others in a way that is soothing, peaceful, and emotionally balanced. For a soulvert, the social environment becomes an extended version of their inner world. It is as though they live in harmony with the energy around them, as if it flows naturally and unobtrusively, filling them with the same quiet energy they would typically find in solitude. This nuanced energy exchange creates a unique social interaction that fosters connection without draining or overwhelming the individual.

The Soulvert's Need for Calmness

Where introverts need alone time to recharge and extroverts seek stimulating social experiences, soulverts seek balance. They do not need to retreat into complete solitude to restore their energy. Still, they do require a peaceful environment where the external energy of others is calm, reflective and non-invasive. The soulvert might be perfectly comfortable spending hours in a library with a small group of people or walking through a serene park with a friend, enjoying the quiet companionship without the need for constant conversation or high-energy engagement.

This preference for tranquillity in the presence of others is key to understanding the soulvert. They need the presence of people to feel alive, but only when the atmosphere allows for a quiet connection. This dynamic interaction can sometimes be complex, as it is less about the spoken word and more about the unspoken bond in a shared, peaceful space. For soulverts, the energy of being around others in a calm, unhurried environment fuels them rather than the external stimulation of conversation or event-driven energy.

Soulverts in the Modern World

Soulverts are often misunderstood or mislabeled in our fast-paced, highly connected world. They are neither strictly introverted nor extroverted, and as such, they may not easily fit into the social frameworks or expectations of the modern world. The frenetic pace of contemporary life, with its constant buzz of activity, overstimulation, and social demands, is often draining for the soulvert. They may find large, noisy social gatherings overwhelming or exhausting, yet struggle in complete isolation. Instead, they crave environments that allow for deep, meaningful presence with others in spaces that offer stillness.

Soulverts often feel like outsiders in a world increasingly designed for extroverts' high-energy, constant interactivity. With its ever-present need for immediate responses and attention, social media may leave them feeling disconnected from others despite being surrounded by a virtual crowd. For the soulvert, this type of interaction is not nourishing but draining. They require quiet spaces, both physical and metaphorical, to connect with the energy of others more subtly and harmoniously.

Yet, the rise of mindful living, meditation, and quiet retreats offers a glimmer of hope for soulverts. These spaces, where people gather for reflection, peaceful conversation, or shared calm experiences, provide an ideal environment for the soulvert to thrive. In these environments, they can recharge in the presence of others without overstimulating the outside world.

The Soulvert's Relationship with Others

The soulvert's energy dynamic is deeply tied to the subtlety of human connection. While extroverts might feel invigorated by an animated conversation or introverts by their alone time, the soulvert thrives on a gentler form of energy exchange. An appreciation marks their interactions for presence over words, calmness over excitement, and peace over chaos. For the soulvert, relationships are not about constant engagement or high-energy interactions; instead, they value shared moments of quiet presence, where the bond is felt not in what is said but in the mere act of being together. This could manifest in sitting with a friend in comfortable silence, engaging in a shared activity like walking or reading or spending time in reflective, meditative companionship. In these moments, the soulvert's energy is replenished, not by the energetic exchange itself, but by the shared, still space in which it takes place.

The Difference between an Ambivert and a Soulvert

An ambivert naturally fluctuates between introversion and extraversion, drawing energy from solitude and social interactions depending on the situation. In contrast, a soulvert is an individual who recharges in the presence of others but only in quiet, serene environments. While an ambivert seeks balance between external engagement and introspection, a soulvert thrives in peaceful social settings, absorbing energy from calm, subtle interactions rather than high-energy or loud environments. Soulverts, unlike ambiverts, prefer tranquillity in social settings to feel rejuvenated, merging the need for connection with a craving for stillness.

The emergence of the soulvert as a new category of human energy brings depth and richness to our understanding of personality and social interaction. These individuals, who are introverts in the sense that they need peace and solitude but who also draw energy from the presence of others in a serene, tranquil environment, offer us a glimpse into the untapped potential of human connection.

To truly honour the soulvert, society must recognise that energy is not always about volume or intensity but is sometimes about the quality of the exchange. The soulvert teaches us that the most profound connections are not always the loudest or most energetic, but rather the quietest, marked by mutual respect, calm, and an unspoken understanding that, sometimes, presence is enough.

Practical Task: Becoming Aware of Your Energy Flow

Step 1: Visualisation of Your Energy

Sit in a quiet space where you won't be disturbed. Close your eyes and take a few deep breaths to centre yourself. Imagine that you are a radiant and powerful source of energy. Visualise yourself glowing with a vibrant, colourful light, any colour that resonates with you, perhaps a golden light, bright white, or a dynamic mix of colours. Feel this energy pulsing through your body, vibrant and alive.

As you breathe deeply, imagine your energy growing stronger with each inhale, becoming more powerful and expansive. With every exhale, feel your energy spreading further outward. Notice how it surrounds you, creating a protective aura of light. Visualise this radiant charge becoming more intense and powerful as you tune into the energy current within you.

Step 2: Assess Where Your Energy is Being Discharged

Now that you can feel your energy's strength, reflect on how it is discharged throughout your day. Visualise your daily activities, interactions, and tasks. Where is your energy being spent? Who are the people or situations that you are interacting with?

Ask yourself:

- Who in my life deserves my precious energy?
- Who drains my energy without offering anything in return?
- What interactions or situations leave me feeling depleted or energised?

As you think about these moments, feel your energy flowing freely or being drawn away. Notice areas where you may give too much to others or engage in situations that drain your reserves.

Step 3: Return to Your Inner Current

Take a moment to return to your centre. Focus on your inner electrical current, the energy always within you, waiting to be tapped. In your mind's eye, imagine that you are reconnecting with your energy source. Visualise the current flowing back into you, recharging your being and restoring balance. Feel your energy becoming replenished, more precise and stronger.

Reflect on how you can prioritise this current:

- How do I wish to give my energy today?
- Where and to whom will I direct my energy?
- What boundaries can I create to protect my energy from those who drain it?

Step 4: Reflect on the People in Your Life

Next, take a moment to think about the people in your life. Visualise the energy that you attract. What type of people are coming into your life? Are they adding positive energy or leaving you feeling drained or unsettled?

Reflect on these questions:

- Am I attracting the kind of energy I desire?
- What kinds of people or experiences am I bringing into my life?
- Are there any patterns of energy exchange that I need to change?

Understand that the energy you emit directly influences the energy you attract. If you want to bring more positive, empowering, and enriching people and experiences into your life, start by healing and evolving your energy. As you grow, develop and align with the energy you wish to receive, you will naturally attract more of that same energy.

Step 5: Evolving Your Energy to Attract What You Desire

Finally, reflect on the aspects of yourself that you need to evolve to attract and receive the energy you desire:

- What parts of myself do I need to heal or grow to acquire the energy I want to receive?

- How can I align my actions, thoughts, and energy with the vibrancy and clarity I wish to attract?
- How can I evolve my mindset to elevate the energy I bring to the world?

Affirmation:

Visualise yourself becoming more aligned with the energy you wish to attract. Imagine your aura expanding, becoming more vibrant and attuning to your desired high-frequency energy. As you grow in strength and clarity, you will naturally begin to see those same qualities reflected in the people and experiences that enter your life.

End this task by grounding yourself. Take a few deep breaths and place your hands over your heart, acknowledging the power and sacredness of your energy. As you open your eyes, be aware of your energy flow throughout the day, knowing you can choose how and where to direct your energy.

Remember, your energy is sacred. By becoming aware of how it flows, who it serves, and how it is replenished, you are taking control of your life's journey, magnetising the experiences and relationships that align with your true essence.

The Silent Gift

Pain after pain, the river flows,
Like a tree of sorrow that does not grow,
The soil is darkened in the night,
The boy passes with a fright,
He drops a seed he did not know,
The roots bond strongly deep down below,
The sun shines on the soil,
They start to form the darkness boils,
New roots take charge, they begin to form,
A tree of light is reborn,
The boy passes that very tree,
He grabs an apple and takes a knee,
He did not recognise the gift he made,
The silent life he had saved.

-KC Palmer

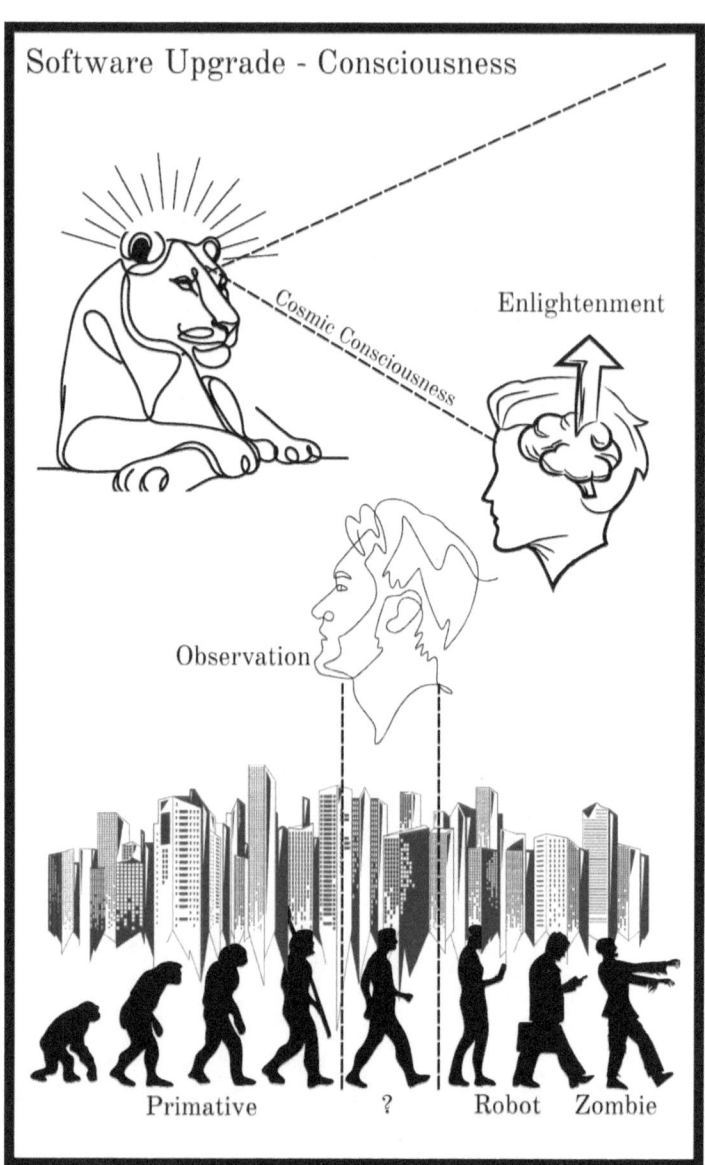

CHAPTER 2
THE HUMAN MIND AND COMPUTER OPERATING SYSTEMS THEORY

THE HUMAN MIND is strikingly like a computer's operating system. Just as a computer requires regular updates, new software, and consistent maintenance to function at its best, so does the human mind. We begin each day with a baseline operating system, our default mental and emotional state.

However, just as a phone or computer doesn't stay the same after its initial setup, neither do we. It is up to us, the user, to choose which programs, updates, and operating systems we download daily. How we interact with the world, what we consume, focus on, and prioritise determines the software we install on our mental hardware.

The Mind as a Task Manager: Managing the Open Tabs

Imagine your mind as a task manager, much like what you find in a computer's operating system. Let's define this function and what it does for those not so technologically savvy.

A computer task manager is a utility that allows users to view and manage running applications, processes, and system performance. It shows active programs and their resource usage (CPU, memory, disk) and allows users to end tasks, troubleshoot issues, and monitor system health. It helps identify and close unresponsive programs, monitor resource usage, and improve system performance. You can access this task manager by pushing CTRL + ALT + DELETE on your computer.

The mind runs multiple programs, thoughts, emotions, memories, tasks, and experiences at any moment. The more tabs we open, the more demands we place on our mental resources. When a computer has 20 tabs open, it slows down, becomes sluggish and may even crash because it can no longer keep up with the demand. The same happens to us when we overload ourselves with too many mental tabs, whether it's stress, anxiety, unresolved issues, or distractions. We lose clarity, mental agility, and the ability to focus on what truly matters.

The solution is simple: we must become aware of the programs running in our minds and manage them effectively. Just as we close unnecessary tabs on a computer to regain speed and efficiency, we must mentally close outdated or irrelevant thoughts, negative patterns, and distractions to clear the mind and make room for higher-level tasks. This requires the practice of mindfulness and self-awareness. By consciously observing our thoughts and letting go of the ones that no longer serve us, we can clear the clutter and perform with greater clarity and focus.

The Elements of the Brain as Computer Hardware

Like computer hardware, the brain has specific functions and components that work together to enable us to operate. A computer's CPU (Central Processing Unit) executes tasks and runs programs. In the human mind, the CPU is akin to the brain, the biological hardware that processes thoughts, perceptions, and information. Our ability to think critically, solve problems, and engage in complex cognitive tasks relies on this mental processing power.

A computer's RAM (Random Access Memory) temporarily holds data the system needs to access quickly. This is like our short-term memory and cognitive functions in the brain. RAM allows us to think on our feet, process information rapidly, and adapt to new situations.

However, just like a computer, the brain has its limits. If too many thoughts are being processed simultaneously or if the RAM is overloaded with unnecessary or negative thoughts, the brain becomes cluttered, leading to mental fatigue and difficulty focusing.

The hard drive in a computer stores long-term data, much like our long-term memory stores experiences, knowledge, and beliefs. This storage capacity determines the software in our minds, including our emotional responses, learned behaviours, and conditioned patterns. If the hard drive is complete with outdated or limiting beliefs, it can slow us down and prevent us from upgrading to a more positive or empowered version of ourselves.

Lastly, a computer's cooling system prevents it from overheating and crashing. In the human mind, this can be compared to consciousness observation, the part of our awareness that observes the mind without judgment. Just as a computer needs to cool down to function correctly, the mind needs time to rest, observe, and let go of unnecessary mental heat. This observation allows us to create distance between ourselves and our thoughts, preventing emotional burnout and cognitive overload.

Zombie Mode: The Baseline Operating System

One of the most significant challenges we face is the tendency to wake up each day and not upgrade our baseline operating system. A term I like to call *zombie mode* describes this experience. When we are in zombie mode, our brains are merely doing the bare minimum to survive. We wake up, eat, work, and sleep, going through the motions on autopilot without actively engaging in life or upgrading our mental state. This is our baseline program, set to keep us functioning, but without much intention or awareness. It's an unconscious loop that has become the default, like a robot programmed to follow a series of commands without deviation.

The mind in zombie mode is on repeat, stuck in an old mental pattern that has learned to prioritise *survival* over *growth*. This zombie state often makes us feel like we live on autopilot, moving through life without deeper engagement, creativity, or emotional fulfilment. We may wake up, repeat the same routine, and fall asleep while never taking the time to consciously evaluate or update our mind's operating system.

The reasons behind this baseline mode are often rooted in societal conditioning. In the 21st century, we live in a world that encourages efficiency, productivity, and consumption. Many of us are trapped in a cycle of unconscious consumption, consuming media, work, and food, without reflection or a genuine connection to our inner selves. Society has shaped this zombie-mode experience in many ways, promoting a system that values doing over being. When people refer to *The Matrix*, I believe this is what they describe: the world that operates automatically, where people are unaware of the potential to upgrade and reprogram their minds for a higher life experience.

> *"If you are unsure, then time is your answer."* – KC Palmer

Upgrading Your Operating System: Downloading the 2.0 Version of Yourself

Like any operating system, the mind can be continually upgraded. Just as a computer software update improves performance, functionality, and security, we, too, can update our mental operating system by engaging in practices that enhance clarity, resilience, and focus.

One way to download your 2.0 software is to align with your true self, connect to your inner purpose, and clear away distractions. Meditation, breathwork, yoga, and any form of exercise are all methods of resetting and recalibrating the mind. These activities help clear mental clutter, improve focus, and reconnect us with our core values and intentions. Much like a computer that benefits from regular updates, the mind benefits from daily practices that enhance self-awareness and mental well-being.

Service and volunteering also play a key role in upgrading the mind. Giving without expectation of return is like downloading a new program that enhances emotional intelligence, compassion, and connection with others. It shifts the focus away from the ego and invites a greater sense of purpose into the mental operating system. By giving to others, we install new software that promotes empathy, kindness, and a deep understanding of fulfillment.

Journaling is another powerful tool for mental upgrades. It allows us to declutter our minds, observe our thoughts, and reflect on our experiences. Just as clearing browser history can help a computer run more efficiently, journaling helps clear the mind and gain insight into our emotional landscape. Finally, gratitude is like anti-virus software for the mind. It protects against negativity, enhances mental resilience and reprograms the brain to focus on the positive. When we practice gratitude, we shift our mental energy from lack to abundance, inviting greater happiness and clarity into our lives.

The human mind is not static; it is a dynamic system that can be upgraded and reprogrammed at will. Each day, we wake up with a baseline operating system, but we must decide which software we will download. We can choose to install outdated, limiting programs, or we can choose to upgrade to a version of ourselves that is more present, more focused and more aligned with our true purpose. By managing our mental task manager, clearing unnecessary mental tabs and downloading practices like meditation, exercise, service, and gratitude, we can unlock our mind's full potential and experience life as a more powerful, agile, and intentional being.

Just as we update our devices to keep them running smoothly, we, too, must upgrade ourselves regularly to keep our minds clear, focused, and capable of handling the demands of life. The power to change, grow, and evolve is always in our hands. Our mental operating system is ours to update at any time. By breaking free from zombie mode and becoming conscious creators of our experiences, we can ensure that our software always reflects the best version of ourselves.

The Art of Emotional Autoregulation: A Path to Conscious Living

Emotions are the invisible currents that shape our reality. They colour our perceptions, guide our decisions, and influence how we interact with the world. Yet, without the ability to autoregulate our emotions, these currents can become storms that can be uncontrollable and destructive. Emotional autoregulation is the unconscious practice of managing and balancing our emotional responses. It is not about suppression but about developing an intimate relationship with our inner world, allowing us to navigate life with greater clarity and purpose.

Emotional autoregulation refers to the ability to monitor, influence, and adjust one's emotional responses in real time. It is the process of recognising our emotional states, understanding their origins, and choosing how to respond rather than react impulsively. This skill is crucial for maintaining mental clarity, fostering emotional resilience, and creating healthy interpersonal relationships. It enables us to hold space for our emotions without becoming overwhelmed or allowing them to dictate our behaviour.

How to Learn Emotional Autoregulation

1. Develop Emotional Awareness: Begin by identifying and naming your emotions as they arise. Regularly check in with yourself throughout the day and notice how you feel without judgment.

2. Pause and Reflect: When strong emotions surface, practice pausing before reacting. This brief moment of reflection allows you to observe your emotional state and choose a more intentional response.

3. Breathing Techniques: Use conscious breathing to regulate your nervous system. Deep, slow breaths help to ground you and bring your body back to a state of calmness.

4. Emotional Journaling: Write about your emotional experiences to process and gain a deeper understanding of them. Journaling provides a reflective space to untangle complex feelings.

5. Practice Mindfulness: Engage in mindfulness meditation to cultivate present-moment awareness. This helps you to stay centered and less reactive when faced with emotional triggers.

6. **Set Healthy Boundaries:** Learn to recognise when external influences drain your energy. Protect your emotional well-being by setting clear boundaries and communicating them assertively.

7. **Self-Compassion:** Treat yourself with kindness when you experience difficult emotions. Acknowledge that emotional responses are natural and part of the human experience.

8. **Seek Feedback:** Engage with trusted friends or mentors who can offer perspective on how you express your emotions and provide support as you refine your regulation skills.

At the heart of emotional autoregulation lies the distinction between emotional dumping and emotional expression. Emotion dumping is the uncontrolled, often unconscious release of feelings onto others without regard for context or the emotional space of the listener. It is reactive, where we seek immediate relief, but often leave a trail of confusion and disconnection. In contrast, expressing emotions is an intentional, conscious act. It involves articulating our feelings in a way that is both honest and respectful. Expression invites connection and understanding, while dumping burdens and overwhelms.

You have learnt about the magnetic pulls and flows in the previous chapter. Ponder here for a second how dumping emotions can make other people feel heavy, confused, or even anxious. Conversely, if you do not establish healthy boundaries, absorbing the unregulated emotions of others can drain your energy, leaving you feeling depleted and disconnected from your own centre. Recognising these dynamics is essential for cultivating emotional balance and protecting your inner equilibrium.

Understanding this distinction is crucial because the way we express our emotions directly impacts our relationships and inner harmony. When we practice emotional autoregulation, we cultivate the ability to pause and reflect before reacting. This pause creates space for discernment, allowing us to identify the root of our emotions, process them internally, and choose how to express them constructively. In doing so, we become more attuned to our inner landscape and less beholden to external triggers.

The journey of consciousness is, at its core, a journey of self-awareness. Emotional autoregulation is a vital part of this journey because our emotional states shape the lens through which we perceive reality. Without regulating our emotions, our thoughts become clouded, and our capacity for clear, reflective insight diminishes. By learning to hold our feelings with presence and care, we refine our ability to observe ourselves without judgment, deepening our reflective practice.

Reflection is not merely the act of looking back—it is the art of looking within. Through emotional autoregulation, we become aware of recurring emotional patterns and the beliefs that underlie them. This awareness is transformative, allowing us to identify areas where we are reactive rather than responsive. Each time we pause to regulate our emotions, we reclaim a piece of our inner sovereignty. In doing so, we begin to break free from unconscious conditioning and align more closely with our higher self.

Moreover, emotional autoregulation fosters emotional resilience. Life is inherently uncertain, and the ability to self-regulate provides a sense of stability amidst the chaos. Rather than being swept away by every emotional wave, we learn to ride them with grace and wisdom. This practice does not make us immune to pain but empowers us to meet it with courage and composure. It allows us to remain open-hearted without being overwhelmed, fostering deeper connections with ourselves and others.

In essence, emotional autoregulation is an act of self-responsibility and self-love. It is a commitment to honouring our emotional experiences while ensuring that our expressions uplift rather than weigh down those around us. As we cultivate this skill, we expand our consciousness, allowing us to engage with life from a place of centeredness and compassion. This, in turn, ripples outward, nurturing a more mindful and harmonious world.

To embark on the path of emotional autoregulation is to choose awareness over autopilot. It is to recognise that our emotions, though powerful, do not define us.

Rather, they are invitations to deepen our understanding of ourselves and the world. By embracing this practice, we not only refine our emotional intelligence but also become active participants in our own evolution, stepping more fully into the truth of who we are.

Boundaries

Boundaries are the sacred lines we draw to honour our essence and protect the integrity of our conscious being. They are not barriers to connection but the architecture of a life lived with intention. Without them, we risk dissolving into the expectations of others, becoming mere shadows of our true selves.

To set a boundary is to declare, "I am here. I exist. I matter." It is an act of self-respect and a profound affirmation of our worth.

When we fail to set boundaries, we relinquish our authority over our own existence. We slip into a passive state—a zombie mode—where our actions are no longer aligned with our internal truth. In this place, we are not living; we are merely surviving, drifting through the currents of other people's desires. This disconnection from our intuitive compass leaves us hollow, drained of the vital energy that makes us magnetic and alive.

To be a people-pleaser is to betray the voice within that whispers our deepest truths. It is to mute the intuitive guidance that exists to steer us toward authenticity and purpose. In seeking external validation, we silence our inner knowing, fragmenting the wholeness of our being. Each time we say "yes" when our soul cries "no," we fracture the sacred bond between our heart and mind. Over time, this fracture drains us of the life force that fuels our creativity, passion, and power.

Boundary setting is also intimately linked to emotional autoregulation—the ability to manage and balance our emotional responses. When we establish clear limits, we create a psychological framework that reduces stress and overwhelming emotions. Boundaries allow us to step back, process our feelings, and respond rather than react. Without them, we become emotionally dysregulated, constantly absorbing and reflecting the energy of those around us. This lack of emotional sovereignty leaves us vulnerable to burnout and inner turmoil. In contrast, healthy boundaries foster a sense of inner stability, empowering us to navigate life's complexities with clarity and calmness.

Here are ten example statements to express boundaries and navigate conversations:

1. I appreciate your perspective, but I need to prioritise my well-being and cannot commit to this right now.
2. I understand your concerns, but I'm not comfortable discussing this topic at the moment.

3. I value our relationship, and to maintain it, I need to set some limits on our communication.
4. I hear you and understand you. However, I do not have the capacity for this conversation right now. I will hold space for you when I'm fully recharged and can give you my full presence.
5. I need some space to process my thoughts. I will reach out when I'm ready to discuss.
6. I respect your opinion, but I need to make decisions that align with my values.
7. I am unable to take on additional responsibilities right now. I hope you understand.
8. I care about you, but I cannot tolerate being spoken to disrespectfully.
9. I need to protect my time and energy, so I won't be able to participate in this event.
10. I'm happy to help within these specific limits, but beyond that, I need to focus on my priorities.

Setting boundaries is not an act of rejection; it is an act of alignment. It is choosing to move through life awake and aware rather than asleep and reactive. When we honour our limits, we cultivate a wellspring of energy that nourishes our highest self. We step into a field of resonance where our presence becomes a magnet for people and experiences that honour who we truly are. This magnetic charge is not born from striving or pleasing but from the authenticity that flows when we live in accordance with our inner compass.

In truth, boundaries are not walls but gateways. They invite others to engage with us from a place of mutual respect and genuine connection. They create the conditions in which our most vibrant selves can thrive. And as we honour ourselves, we permit others to do the same—to step out of zombie mode and into the fullness of their conscious being. Setting a boundary is about reclaiming your voice, intuition, and power. It is a radical act of self-love and a declaration that your presence is sacred. In this commitment to yourself, you awaken from the numbness of people-pleasing and emerge as a force of clarity, vitality, and truth.

Embarking on the path of consciousness is an inherently solo endeavour. No one else can wake you up. As you begin to observe your thoughts and dismantle long-held beliefs, you are, in essence, unravelling years of conditioning. This is not an easy process. It requires courage to confront the narratives you have lived by and the willingness to rewire your mind. Every struggle, every relationship and every opportunity becomes a mirror reflecting aspects of yourself. The outer world is a projection of your inner world, and as you become more conscious, you will begin to decipher these reflections. This process is ongoing. There is no final destination, only a continual unfolding into greater clarity and self-awareness.

In our modern world, advice is given freely and frequently. From social media to casual conversations, it is easy to be inundated with opinions on how to live your life. Yet, advice should be regarded as sacred. Words have the power to alter the trajectory of someone's path. Before offering guidance, ask yourself:

- Is this advice rooted in my own conditioning or unhealed trauma?
- Am I speaking from a place of clarity and regulation?
- Is my perspective objective, or is it coloured by my personal experiences?

Equally important is discerning the advice you receive. Not all guidance is created equally. Consider whether the person offering it is grounded, capable of self-regulation, and free from projection. Ultimately, the responsibility for exploring and evaluating advice rests with you.

When did we lose our ability to trust our understanding? There was a time when decisions were made through quiet introspection and deep self-inquiry. In today's fast-paced, hyper-connected society, the impulse to seek external validation often overrides our innate wisdom. It is easier to type a question into a search engine than to sit quietly and allow the answer to arise from within.

However, your intuitive power remains intact. It has been buried beneath layers of noise and distraction. To reclaim it, begin by cultivating silence, observing your inner landscape, and trusting the subtle wisdom that emerges. Your consciousness is a living, breathing guide that, once tuned into, can illuminate the path ahead. The journey to awareness is yours alone to walk. With patience and practice, you will begin to see beyond the surface of life and touch the essence of who you truly are.

Practical Task:
Clearing Your Mental Task Manager

Step 1: Visualise Your Mind as a Control Centre

Close your eyes and take a few deep breaths. Imagine your mind as a control centre or a task manager window. Visualise this task manager screen in your mind, where each tab represents a task, appointment, responsibility, or recurring thought that occupies your mental space. These tabs might represent work tasks, personal responsibilities, emotional concerns, or ongoing worries. See how many tabs are open; there may be many, some overlapping or running in the background without you even realising it.

Step 2: Write Down Your Tabs

Open your eyes and grab a notebook or piece of paper. Start by writing down all the tabs you have open in your mind. These can be anything that you feel mentally responsible for, whether it's:

- Work tasks or projects
- Appointments or deadlines
- Personal relationships, concerns, or ongoing commitments
- Reoccurring thoughts, worries, or mental patterns
- Unfinished tasks or unresolved emotions

Write down everything that comes to mind without filtering. Don't worry about the order; get everything out of your head and onto paper. This is your mental task list or inventory of what demands your attention.

Step 3: Zoom Out and Assess Your Mental Load

Now, take a step back and look at your list. Imagine you're zooming out of your control centre, seeing all the open tabs before you. This gives you a broader perspective of what your mind is handling daily. Consider:

- How many of these tabs are necessary or urgent?
- How many tasks or thoughts have run in the background, draining energy without much action or resolution?
- Which tabs are habitual thoughts or recurring worries that may not need immediate attention?

Notice how this mental load feels, perhaps overwhelming, scattered, or cluttered. Recognising how much your mind is processing at once can be a powerful realisation of how much energy you're using unconsciously.

Step 4: Prioritize the Important Tasks

Now, look at your list and prioritise. Which tasks or thoughts truly matter? What is in line with your higher self and your purpose? Write down the most important or urgent tasks at the top of the page. These are the things that align with your goals, your values, and your well-being. These should be the areas that receive your energy and attention first.

For example:

- Important Work Projects
- Health and Self-Care
- Relationships that Need Attention or Nurturing
- Personal Growth and Development Goals
- Upcoming Commitments or Appointments

Your priority tabs need your focus and active engagement.

Step 5: Delete or End Tasks That Don't Serve You

Once you've identified what truly matters, it's time to clear out the tabs that no longer serve your higher self. These might be tasks that are lingering, outdated, or things you feel obligated to do but that don't align with your true purpose. Consider closing or deleting unnecessary tabs from your mental task manager.

Step 6: Practice Ongoing Maintenance

As you regularly check your phone or computer to see which apps or programs are running in the background, it's important to practice maintaining your mental task manager. Throughout the week, whenever you feel overwhelmed or scattered, take a moment to do a quick mental check-in. See what tabs are still open and re-prioritise accordingly. Delete or close any tasks that no longer serve you and affirm your commitment to focusing only on what aligns with your higher purpose.

Remember, you are the task manager of your mind. You have the power to control what occupies your mental space. By choosing which tasks deserve your energy and attention, you can live with greater focus, clarity and intention. Keep your mental space clear and only allow the tasks that serve your highest self to run in the foreground of your life.

As you mentally close each unnecessary task or thought, repeat the following affirmation to solidify your intention:

Affirmation:

"I choose to remove this task or thought from my entirety. I prioritise functions that align with my true self and serve my higher purpose." Visualise each tab disappearing from your mind. As they close, feel the weight lifting from your mental space. Notice how your mind feels lighter, more transparent and more focused. Trust that you've made room for what truly matters.

"Remember, the decisions you make are based on the information available to you at the time. One cannot doubt or regret such choices with the benefit of hindsight. The present moment is all we have; only fools contemplate beyond." – KC Palmer

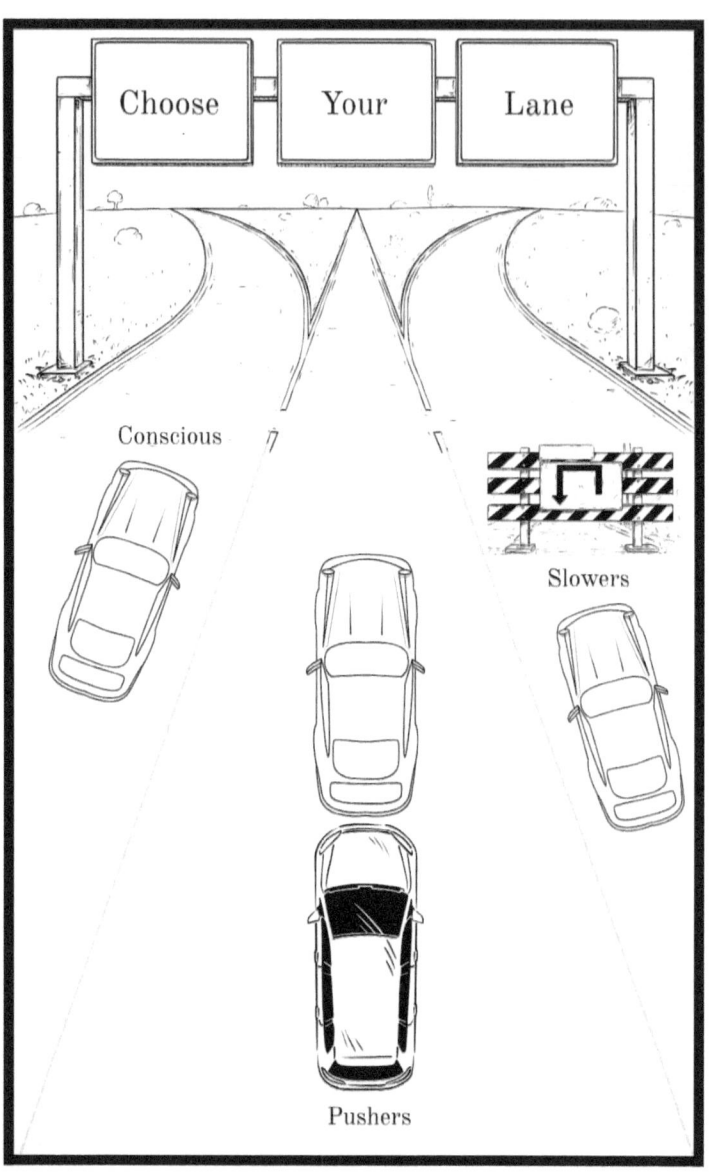

CHAPTER 3
THE HIGHWAY OF LIFE

"Stop doing and start being. Stop chasing the frantic pace of social conditioning. It's time you choose your own speed and appreciate the simplicity of just being. People naturally open themselves to abundance and greater offerings when they express gratitude at this level. Then one shall receive life's universal signs and messages effortlessly." – KC Palmer

HUMANITY IS NOW travelling at unprecedented speeds. For most of history, our movement was limited to the pace of our own feet, the gallop of a horse, or the steady rhythm of wind in a ship's sails. Then, almost overnight, we broke these boundaries. Automobiles, aeroplanes, and rockets pushed us past the horizon, compressing distances and transforming the very essence of time.

The arrival of the internet introduced an even greater acceleration, with instantaneous information transfer and a rewiring of human consciousness. It's been just over a century since the Wright brothers achieved flight, and barely twenty-five years since broadband internet connected us in previously unimaginable ways.

However, amidst this rapid advancement, something crucial has been lost. We have become conditioned to expect speed, wired to demand everything be faster, more efficient, and optimised. In doing so, we have built a world that struggles to slow down. We gauge our days not by experiences but by outputs, our value not by depth but by productivity. Rest feels like wasted time, and stillness feels like stagnation.

The modern world demands urgency, prompt replies, immediate results, and a relentless pursuit of achievements. Even our relaxation is filled with stimuli; our minds cannot tolerate silence without reaching for a screen, distraction, or escape.

This relentless pace has not led to greater fulfilment; it has left us restless. We no longer navigate life, we sprint, pursuing goals that outpace us. We scroll through our lives at lightning speed, consuming without digesting and experiencing without reflection. We have lost the ability to be present in our rush to move forward.

Life is like a vast highway, full of different lanes, speeds, and obstacles. The way we navigate this highway profoundly impacts our experience of life. The lanes we choose, the speed at which we drive, and how we react to the actions of others all shape the flow of our journey. Our conscious choices in these moments can lead to a peaceful, fulfilling experience or to frustration and stress. Just like driving on a physical highway, the lanes we take reflect how we approach life, with each lane representing a different pace, mindset, or approach to the world.

The Three Drivers of Life: Navigating the Road of Existence

How we drive reflects how we live. Some force their way forward, some hold others back, and some flow, unbothered, navigating freely. Throughout my own journey, I have identified three main types of drivers.

The Pusher: The Relentless Chaser

This driver is always in a hurry, tailgating, honking and weaving through traffic as if the road belongs to them alone. Their existence is defined by the illusion of time and the need to be ahead at all costs. They mistake movement for progress and speed for success. They see others not as fellow travellers but as obstacles, barriers to their relentless pursuit of first. But they fail to realise that the road stretches endlessly before them. There is no actual finish line, only the illusion of one, ever-moving, always out of reach. Their need to push ahead closes their eyes to the journey, leaving them exhausted, frustrated, and forever chasing a destination they will never truly reach.

The Slow-Downer: The Roadblock to Growth

Some sit idly in the lane, oblivious to the flow of movement around them. Distracted, unbothered, and often indifferent, they unknowingly slow the progress of those behind them. Not because they are intentionally malicious but because they do not recognise, or refuse to accept, that others have their own pace and path to follow. To them, someone else's momentum is a threat. If another car moves swiftly and purposefully, it unsettles their static existence. Instead of stepping aside, they remain in the way, blocking progress, unconsciously keeping others stuck in their rhythm of inaction.

The Flow-er: The Master of the Road

And then, there is the one who flows. The driver who reads the road senses the rhythm of movement and adapts effortlessly. They do not force their way forward, nor do they hinder others. Instead, they navigate with awareness, shifting lanes, allowing the pushers to rush ahead and move around the slow-downers without frustration. The flower understands that the road is not about control but about balance. They know when to accelerate and when to ease off, when to hold their ground and when to yield.

The speed of others does not define their journey, instead using their internal compass and ability to move in harmony with life. Life does not force us to stay in one lane forever. We have the power to shift, to choose how we move. If we race unthinkingly ahead, we may burn out before we arrive. If we refuse to move at all, we may be left behind. But if we learn to flow and read the energy of life as we do the road, we can travel with purpose, presence, and peace. Ultimately, the journey is not about who gets there first or stopping others from moving forward. It is about how well we navigate our own sacred road, how deeply we experience the ride, and how effortlessly we learn to flow.

The Power of Control: Navigating with Awareness

The beauty of being on your highway of life is that you have the wheel. You are in complete control. The moment we react with anger or change lanes without thinking, we begin to lose that control. When we allow our emotions to dictate our actions, whether on the road or in life, we face problems. The key to a smooth journey lies in remaining conscious of our decisions, staying aware of our surroundings and choosing our path intentionally.

When someone cuts us off or when we feel like we're being rushed, it's essential to take a deep breath and reassess. Often, the most peaceful course of action is to create space. When we're tailgated, instead of speeding up or getting frustrated, the simplest solution might be to change lanes and let them pass. This resolves the immediate conflict and helps preserve our emotional energy for the things that matter. The faster we rush, the more we risk losing control.

Relationships: The Shared Highway, Separate Lanes

In relationships, whether romantic, platonic, or familial, we each have our lane. While it's essential to travel the same highway, having shared values and goals, it's equally important to honour that each person's journey will unfold at their own pace. Just as two drivers might travel together on the same road but at different speeds, it's essential to recognise that your partner or loved ones may move at a different pace.

This doesn't mean they are on a separate path; their lane may require different timing. In relationships, the key is alignment, not synchronisation. You and your partner may have different speeds, but you move in the same direction if your destinations align. You must allow space for one another's lanes and honour each other's pace, not forcing or rushing the other to match yours.

Focus on Your Journey: Avoiding Comparison and Ego

It's easy to get distracted by the lanes of others, but this can lead to unnecessary stress and dissatisfaction. When you focus too much on the speed at which others are travelling or try to match their pace, you risk losing sight of your path. It's essential to focus on your journey, understanding that your lane may look different from others, and that's okay.

Life is not a race; it's a journey you can experience at your own pace. By staying focused on your journey without comparing yourself to others, you preserve your energy and control your experience. Guide others when needed, but don't rush them, and don't force them into your lane. Respect their flow, just as you hope they respect yours.

> "A caterpillar does not concern itself with the colour of its wings." – KC Palmer

Life resembles a road on which we often encounter potholes—deep, rugged holes that disrupt our comfort and shatter the illusion of steady progress. These potholes symbolise our struggles, harmful habits, and unresolved traumas. When faced with them, our instinct is to fill them swiftly, patch them up, and move on as if they weren't there.

The quick fix appears inviting, a distraction or a temporary remedy, providing a comforting illusion of resolution. However, like a road patched hastily, this fix remains superficial. When challenges arise, the water seeps in, undermining the foundation, the potholes resurface, often worse than before. This repetitive cycle keeps us dodging, stumbling and grappling with the same issues.

Yet, there's a different approach. Instead of merely patching up a damaged path, we can create a new one, built on patience, understanding, and substantial change. This demands effort, time, and a commitment to dismantle old habits rather than conceal them. It requires us to avoid the potholes and understand their origins. Creating a new road necessitates dedication to profound, intentional change. It involves unlearning detrimental behaviours and establishing a more robust foundation.

This endeavour is neither quick nor easy. It calls for excavating the unstable ground, confronting discomfort, and resisting shortcuts. However, once this new road is established, the journey flows smoothly. We no longer brace for unexpected bumps or fear cracks resurfacing beneath us. We can proceed confidently, assured that our road is built to endure.

Genuine change is not about temporary fixes; it is about complete reconstruction. We can persist in patching the same road or invest time in building one that supports us with resilience, stability, and tranquillity. The highway of life is filled with choices, from the lanes we choose to the speed at which we travel. By navigating with consciousness and awareness, we can avoid road rage, unnecessary stress, and frustration.

You are the driver of your life. Choose your lane, set your speed and remain focused on your journey. Don't be distracted by others rushing or tailgating; instead, honour your own pace. By consciously choosing your lane and navigating life with mindfulness, you'll experience greater peace, control, and clarity. When we consciously choose our pace and direction, we unlock the freedom to travel with intention, purpose and flow.

Practical Task:
Choose Your Lane with Consciousness

Step 1: Evaluate Your Current Lane and Speed

Take a few moments to reflect on your current pace and direction in life. Are you moving too fast, feeling rushed or overwhelmed? Or are you moving slowly, with intention and mindfulness?

Write down your current goals and responsibilities. Are you consciously choosing the speed at which you're working, or are external pressures influencing you? Assess if you need to adjust your pace or shift to a different lane (slower or faster) to better align with your current needs.

Step 2: Practice Mindful Driving

Practice mindfulness while driving or doing other daily activities for a day. This can be especially useful when you're feeling rushed or frustrated. When faced with traffic or someone cutting you off, consciously take a deep breath, focus on staying calm and respond thoughtfully. Notice how your reactions change when you slow down instead of reacting instantly.

Step 3: Create Space in Your Life

Evaluate your boundaries with work, social commitments, or relationships. Are you feeling tailgated or crowded by external expectations? Identify at least one area where you can create more space by saying no, asking for help, or simply scheduling personal time. Making room for yourself allows for a smoother, more peaceful journey.

Step 4: Reflect on Your Relationships and Their Lane

Think about your closest relationships and how you approach them. Are you trying to rush someone else's journey, or is there room to honour their pace? Contact a partner, friend, or family member and ask about their current path or speed. Reflect on how you can support them without trying to sync your pace entirely with theirs.

Step 5: Avoid the Comparison Trap

Reflect on how often you compare your pace or progress to others. Does this lead to stress or dissatisfaction? Practice focusing on your journey for one week rather than comparing it to others. If you think about someone else's progress, gently shift your focus to your goals, values, and unique path.

Step 6: Set an Intentional Direction

Set a clear intention for the next phase of your life, whether it's related to career, personal growth, or relationships. Write down key goals you want to work toward. Are you consciously choosing the right lane for these goals? Break them down into actionable steps and regularly check if your actions are aligned with the direction you've set.

Step 7: Mindful Lane Changes

Identify moments when you've had to change lanes due to external pressure or internal shifts. How did you navigate these transitions? Were you conscious or reactive in your decision? Reflect on the last significant life change or transition you faced. How did you handle it? In hindsight, would you have handled it differently? Write about how you could have navigated the situation with more mindfulness and intentionality.

Step 8: Control Your Emotional Reactions

Practice consciously controlling your emotional reactions when something negatively triggers you. In moments of frustration (whether on the road or in life), pause for a few seconds before reacting. Try to think of a solution or a calmer response that maintains your peace rather than escalating the situation.

Step 9: Daily Reflection on Your Pace

At the end of each day, reflect on your pace and how you navigated the day. Did you rush through things? Were you mindful and intentional with your choices? Journal about your day's pace. Were there moments when you felt overwhelmed or out of control? How can you adjust your pace tomorrow to align with your needs?

Step 10: Create a Roadmap for Your Future

Visualise where you want to be in the next few years. Where are you heading on your highway of life? Create a roadmap or vision board for your future. What lanes will you choose? Will you move fast or slow? Make sure your roadmap reflects your values and goals, and commit to revisiting it regularly to ensure you're still headed in the right direction.

Affirmation:

I am the conscious driver of my life, choosing my lane with intention and wisdom. I trust my pace, honouring both my journey and the journeys of others. I move with clarity, creating space for peace and reflection. I release comparison and embrace my unique path. With each decision, I flow with awareness, guided by love, patience, and mindfulness. I remain centred, knowing that I can navigate any road with grace and ease, moving forward with purpose and trust in the process of life.

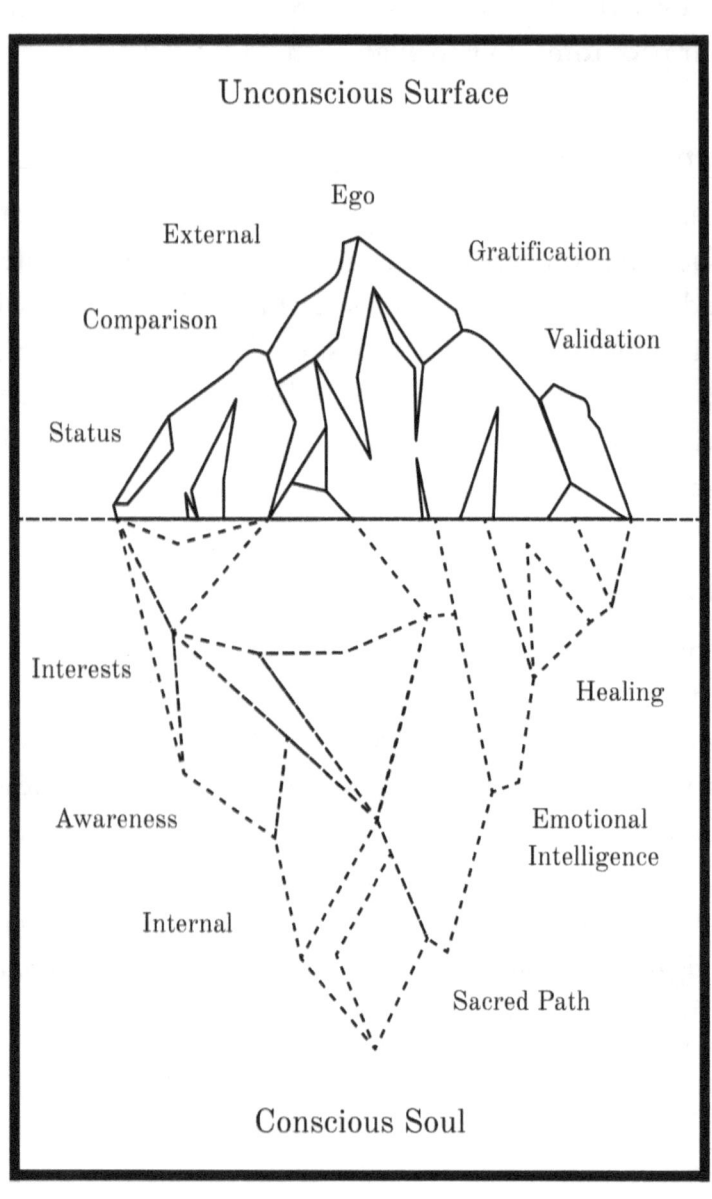

CHAPTER 4
THE ICEBERG OF TRUE CONNECTION

"The eyes are the gateway to the mind; close them and you'll find the path to your soul." – KC Palmer

AT THE SURFACE of every individual lies an external shell, our physical appearance, habits, behaviours, and the image we present to the world. Much like the tip of an iceberg, this outer layer is what others most often perceive of us. It's what we show at first glance or when interacting with others.

But just as an iceberg's accurate mass is submerged beneath the surface, so too is the depth of who we are, including our emotions, beliefs, dreams, traumas, and soul's journey. Most of our being lies hidden from view, and only through authentic connection and unconditional acceptance can we truly understand one another's depth.

The Tip of the Iceberg vs. the Depths of the Soul

The tip of the iceberg represents everything visible: our physical body, social persona, and online presence. It's what people judge first and often, it's all they get to see. It lacks depth and fails to reflect the complexities that lie beneath. When we look at a person, whether a partner, friend, or stranger, we only witness the tip of their iceberg, the most surface-level layer of their being. True love and connection, however, can only be found when two people are willing to dive beneath that surface and see the true depths of each other's being. This brings us to a typical relationship struggle: Why don't they undersand me?

When we feel misunderstood or unseen by someone, it often stems from an incompatibility with each other's depths. This issue arises not from the lack of love but from the fact that the other person may not have the emotional, mental, or spiritual capacity to comprehend the full scope of who we are. Their iceberg may not extend as deeply as ours, so they can't see or hear the layers that make us who we are. This doesn't make either person wrong or less worthy; it speaks to the differences in the layers of the two people's souls and journeys.It's possible to be in a relationship with someone whose iceberg is smaller or less complex. Perhaps they are still in the process of growing, learning, and understanding their depths. In such relationships, there is an opportunity for growth. One partner can guide, motivate, and encourage the other to dive deeper into themselves, open more layers, and explore their proper depths.

Doing this with love, patience, and respect can lead to a powerful dynamic where individuals grow and evolve together. However, this doesn't mean the relationship will always be easy or seamless. Suppose there is significant friction, misunderstanding, or disconnection. In that case, it's essential to reflect on whether the icebergs are from the same ice sheet, meaning, whether the two individuals are aligned in their journeys, growth, and emotional capacity. Genuine connection is based on the ability to see and appreciate the deeper layers of one another, and sometimes, the dissonance comes from one person being too deep for the other to understand or vice versa.

Human attraction is often seen as a mystery of chemistry, a fusion of energies that pull us toward another. Yet, beneath the surface of our connections, there is usually an unseen force at play, a pull not of love but of recognition. It is the recognition of the wounds we carry, the missing pieces we subconsciously attempt to reclaim through others. When trauma bonding arises in relationships, it often reveals itself through cycles of seeking and unmasking, through the illusion of completeness shattered by the surfacing of wounds yet to be healed.

The following is an example of a mature masculine with an immature feminine profile:

Perhaps, in our upbringing, we were only taught one half of ourselves. Maybe we were moulded into a rigid masculine frame, instilled with discipline, logic, and control, but were never taught the gentle embrace of the feminine, the fluidity, the receptivity, the nurturing essence that soothes the soul. So, we seek it elsewhere. We are drawn to beauty, softness, and a grace that seems foreign yet longed for.

At first, this woman, this embodiment of the feminine, seems to complete us. She is the missing thread that weaves through the cracks in our being. But as we peel back her layers and hold her in vulnerability, we find she is wounded too. The softness we sought contains its pain, its history of survival. And if we are not whole within ourselves, we enter an endless cycle, seeking, never truly healing, and only repeating.

Thus, only when we explore and heal the depths of the masculine and feminine do we truly find internal balance and alignment within relationships.

It is important for me to note here that this is one specific imbalance of the several circumstances we can find ourselves in. To dive into each scenario would require a whole other book, which may be written in the future. However, for now, there are unlimited resources to google, watch, or read, which will deepen your iceberg and ultimately develop your understanding of human behaviour.

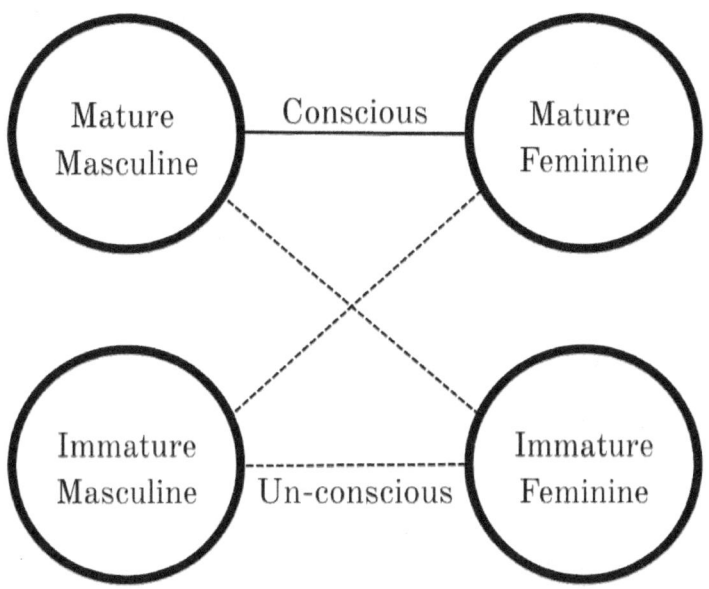

The Archetypes: Immature and Mature Masculine & Feminine

To truly understand these patterns, we must explore the nature of the energies we embody. The immature masculine is control-driven, fearful of vulnerability, and seeks power through external validation. It does not trust the feminine, seeing it as chaotic or weak. It dominates or withdraws, unable to hold space for actual emotional depth.

Conversely, the mature masculine is centred, grounded, and harmonious with power and compassion. It does not seek completion through another but instead offers strength in presence. It protects without controlling, leads without oppressing, and honours the feminine as an equal counterpart.

The immature feminine is reactive, seeking security through attachment, often manifesting in co-dependence. It can be manipulative, using emotion as a weapon or means of control, usually fearing abandonment above all else. It seeks the masculine not for partnership, but for salvation.

The mature feminine, however, is sovereign in her being. She is receptive yet assertive, nurturing yet holds her boundaries. She does not seek the masculine to complete her, but to dance harmoniously with her. She trusts herself, and in that trust, she allows for a partnership built on mutual respect rather than hidden wounds.

So, what does this mean for us as individuals navigating relationships? It means that before we reach outward, we must look inward. If we do not know what lies beneath our surface, our wounds, our fears, our unconscious patterns, then we will forever be caught in the seeking cycle, mistaking trauma familiarity for love.

To truly recognise a partner and build a connection beyond the wounds, we must first integrate the lost parts of ourselves. We must become aware of our inner feminine and masculine, cultivate them in maturity and stand whole in our being. Only then can we see a partner not as a missing piece, but as a reflection of our wholeness. Love is not found in another's arms but in the depths of one's soul. Only when we have seen ourselves fully can we truly see another.

The Impact of Technology on Depth

In the 21st century, we are constantly presented with the idea of superficial connection, primarily fuelled by technology and social media. Platforms like Instagram, dating apps, and online profiles often prioritise the external tip of the iceberg using perfect selfies, curated photos, and idealised personas. People advertise their physicality, surface-level accomplishments, and perfect lives in a way that may draw attention.

Still, these representations often don't reflect the depth of the person behind the screen. In online dating, for example, people frequently use their shells to attract a partner, posting seductive photos to gain attention, yet still desiring a deep, emotional connection. This creates a paradox: how can one seek someone who connects with their soul while only showing their outer layers?

The energy one projects into the world through these platforms becomes a magnet, drawing in others attracted to that same surface energy. But just as magnets of incompatible charges will repel each other, so will individuals whose depths don't align. What you attract is often a reflection of the energy you are putting out. When considering the Magnet Theory in Chapter 1, we can reflect on how the energy we project through our iceberg tip impacts the type of people we attract into our lives.

Suppose we focus primarily on attracting attention to our physical shell. In that case, we may magnetise individuals who are also mainly interested in superficial traits, those who are attracted only to the external and who don't have the capacity or desire to explore deeper layers.

This raises an important question: *What is the purpose of the energy you are putting out into the world?* Are you projecting a reflection of who you are, or are you simply engaging in surface-level connections in hopes of validation or attention? To attract someone who sees your true self, you must align your energy with the depth and authenticity you seek. If your energy remains on the surface, so will the relationships you attract.

Proper connection and love are found when two people can see, appreciate, and love the depths of each other's icebergs. This requires vulnerability, willingness to explore and the ability to accept and understand the complexities of the other's soul. Recognising that not everyone can see or appreciate your full depth is essential, and that's okay.

But in relationships, knowing whether your depths align and whether you are ready and willing to explore and grow together is crucial. In a world obsessed with the outer shell, we must ask ourselves: Are we projecting only the tip of the iceberg, or are we opening the depths of our being to those who can truly see us for who we are? True love doesn't lie on the surface; it exists in the shared sacred journey of understanding each other's layers.

Modern society has become a house of mirrors, obsessed with its reflection yet terrified of what lies beyond the surface. We polish the glass, perfect the angles, and manipulate the lighting to ensure that the image looking back at us is flawless. Yet, beneath this carefully curated exterior, something vital is missing. We have become a species more concerned with how we *appear* than how we *are*, mistaking the mirror for the self and the reflection for reality.

We are conditioned to refine our outer shell from the moment we wake. We sculpt our bodies, tailor our identities, and filter our lives through digital frames, ensuring every imperfection is smoothed. We measure success not by the richness of our inner world but by how others perceive us via likes and comments, which determine our value and the admiration of strangers. We live on the surface, mistaking the skin for the soul, the applause for fulfilment.

But mirrors only show us what is external. They reflect light, not depth. To honestly know oneself, one must step beyond the illusion, past the gleaming veneer of perfection and into the depths behind the eyes, where absolute truth resides. Yet, this is the journey modern society fears most. It is easier to keep refining the reflection than to face what lurks beneath.

Within that depth lies the raw, unfiltered self, the insecurities, contradictions, and wounds we have buried beneath layers of presentation. Looking inward requires courage, for it is in that darkness that the fundamental transformation begins, not in the sculpted body or the admired image but in the quiet confrontation of what lies beneath.

The quest for meaning does not begin in the mirror. It starts when we turn away from it, stop chasing perfection, and embrace the depth of our being. Only then do we move beyond the illusion, the shallow waters of perception and into the vast, uncharted depths of the self.

Practical Task: Exploring Your Iceberg; Honouring Your Depths

Step 1: Visualise Yourself as a Magnificent Iceberg

Close your eyes and take a few deep breaths to centre yourself. Imagine you are a grand iceberg floating in the vast, calm Arctic Sea. See your iceberg's outer shell, the tip that rises above the water, representing your physical form, the external persona you show to the world. This is the surface level of who you are: your body, your appearance, your social mask, and the image others might first encounter.

Step 2: Honour Your Internal Beauty

Now, allow your awareness to descend beneath the surface into the deep, expansive layers of your iceberg that lie submerged in the water. These hidden depths represent the true beauty and complexity of your being: your thoughts, feelings, desires, experiences, wisdom, struggles, and soul's purpose. Recognise the intricate layers within you, each one unique and full of meaning. Take a moment to honour this internal beauty, this sacred and powerful essence that is yours and yours alone.

Step 3: Reflect on Your Relationships

Now, bring your awareness to the people in your life, friends, family, colleagues, or partner. Consider how they interact with your iceberg:

- Do they see and appreciate your depth?
- How do you represent your iceberg to these people?
- Are you allowing them to witness the actual layers of your being, or are you only showing them the surface?

Take time to reflect on these questions. Notice how these people engage with you. Are they interested in your full depth, or are they only connecting with your outer shell? Recognise if there is an imbalance between how much of yourself you share versus how much others are able or willing to see.

Step 4: Decide Who Sees Your Depth

This step lets you make an intentional choice about who gets to see your entire iceberg and how much of your depths you wish to reveal. You might decide that certain people have earned the privilege to understand your deeper layers, while others may only ever see the surface. Remember, it's okay to have boundaries, and not everyone needs to have access to your entire iceberg. You have the power to decide.

Reflect on the relationships that nourish you and allow your depth to be seen versus those that might only interact with your outer shell. Consider how you will honour and protect the sacred layers of your soul moving forward.

Step 5: Moving Forward

As you move through your day, carry the awareness of your iceberg with you. Make decisions based on your deepest layers, not just your external shell. Honour your soul's journey and remember that you are worthy of being seen in your full complexity by those ready to embrace it.

This task is an ongoing practice, just as an iceberg continuously moves through the sea, your depth constantly evolves. Allow yourself to honour that journey with love, respect and consciousness.

Affirmation:

"I honour my internal sacred soul. My external shell is my soul's physical form in this life. I will use my physical form to make decisions and follow a path of purity and love to my higher self."

Feel the truth of this affirmation resonate through your being. Acknowledge that your external shell is a tool, a vehicle, through which you navigate this life, but it does not define you. Your true essence is far more profound, and you have the right to decide how and with whom you share that depth.

Seeking Moth

Low Vibration

Accepting Flame

High Vibration

CHAPTER 5
THE MOTH AND THE FLAME – THE DANCE BETWEEN SEEKING AND BEING

"What is my purpose? What am I here for? First, you must transform yourself into a beacon of light; then, the answers will shine through the darkness."

IN THE QUIET spaces of our lives, there lies a profound and ancient dance, one between the moth and the flame. It is not just a natural occurrence but a metaphor that speaks to the human condition, the nature of desire, the pursuit of external validation, and the path to self-actualisation.

In its frantic fluttering, the moth represents the part of us constantly seeking, chasing after fleeting sources of light, excitement, and external approval. It moves from one distraction to another, driven by the promise of something beyond itself. The flame, on the other hand, is rooted, strong, and centred. It does not chase the moth; it simply burns with a light so fierce and steady that it is naturally drawn to it, yet it remains unperturbed. The moth desires to consume, to burn brightly for a moment, to be seen, while the flame is eternal, glowing with the certainty of its existence.

The Moth

The moth is symbolic of the human tendency to seek external validation. It is driven by an incessant longing to be recognised, admired, or approved of. It has no centre of its own, so it flies in pursuit of any flame that promises to give it significance. It flutters through the night, lost in the desire for something outside of itself, chasing the light, intoxicated by its glow, often unaware of the danger it faces in its pursuit.

In this analogy, the flame represents the approval of others, the fleeting recognition or the pursuit of hollow distractions that offer no lasting fulfilment. This chasing behaviour stems from an inherent emptiness, a deep sense of ungroundedness. The moth seeks to fill this void by constantly flying from one thing to another. Whether it's social media, external praise, a new relationship, or an endless stream of entertainment, the moth believes that reaching for the next shining thing will find satisfaction, a sense of worth, or a sense of purpose.

But just as the moth's desire for the flame leads it to destruction, so does the pursuit of external validation, eventually leading to a loss of self. The moth's flight is erratic, chaotic, and unsustainable. It is constantly distracted, forever needing the approval of others to feel alive, to feel seen and important. This is the path of instability: continuous movement between distractions, the inability to stay still, and the belief that happiness or purpose lies in something external. But no matter how many flames the moth visits, it never finds peace. Instead, it leaves behind a trail of burnt wings, a life of exhaustion, and a soul wounded in pursuit of a mirage.

The Flame

In contrast, the flame represents something more profound, the quiet strength of being centred on one's essence. A flame does not chase after anything; it simply burns with a steady, unwavering light. It is grounded in its existence, needing no validation or external source of recognition to affirm its worth.

The flame symbolises a soul in complete alignment with its purpose. This soul has discovered its true nature and shines brightly and unapologetically into the world from that space of knowing. A flame does not need to seek attention or approval. It burns for itself, not to be seen, but because it is simply its nature to do so. It radiates outward, not to manipulate or control, but because it is.

The flame attracts those seeking light in its radiance, just as a centred individual attracts others through their authenticity, sense of purpose, and strength. It is not a quest for validation but a peaceful, focused burning of truth.

This flame is not simply a light in the dark; it is the manifestation of a soul that fully aligns with its deepest values and its true path. The flame is unwavering in its journey, even when the moths come, drawn to its light. The moths may circle and attempt to consume the flame, but the flame remains untouched, unbothered by the external noise. The flame does not need to change its nature to accommodate the moths. It continues to burn, shining radiance that cannot be dulled by fleeting distractions or the empty desire for approval.

The flame knows its purpose is not to entertain or please but to illuminate, guide, and stand as a testament to what it means to be true to oneself. The moths may come and go, but the flame's essence is eternal. It does not need to chase; it simply burns.

The Dance Between the Moth and the Flame

The dance between the moth and the flame is an age-old allegory for the struggle between seeking and being.

The moth reflects the ego, pursuing what it believes will make it whole: status, recognition, or external approval. The flame is the soul, firm in its authenticity, steadfast in its purpose and content in its light. The moth flies from one flame to another, desperate to be seen, validated, and feel significant. But it is the flame that remains undisturbed, glowing brightly from within.

This is not to say that the moth is inherently wrong or that seeking is a flaw. Pursuing external validation can be a natural part of the human experience. However, the key difference lies in the awareness of what one is chasing and why. A life spent endlessly chasing external approval leads to exhaustion and disillusionment. In contrast, a life lived as a flame, grounded in purpose, allows one to shine without needing to search for anything outside oneself.

To be the flame is to recognise that everything you need is already within you. It is to stand in your truth, to align with your deepest values, and to trust that in doing so, you will attract those who are meant to come into your life, not because you seek their approval but because your light resonates with theirs. The flame does not chase the moth; it simply burns, knowing its purpose is more significant than any fleeting validation.

Becoming the Flame

The journey from being a moth to becoming a flame is going from instability to wholeness. It is the path of self-discovery, of realising that true fulfilment does not lie in external approval or distractions but in the unwavering connection to one's inner essence. To be the flame is to burn with a fierceness that comes from being fully aligned with your soul's purpose, without fear, hesitation, and the need for anything or anyone to validate your existence. The moth may seek many flames, but only the one who burns with truth, authenticity, and a deep inner alignment will shine brightly enough to light the way.

As we let go of the frantic chasing, we allow ourselves to become that strong, centred, and eternal flame, inviting all the moths ready to find their way home.

In the final stages of realisation or spiritual evolution, two flames, each strong, grounded, and burning brightly with their unique light, can form a powerful and sacred union. Having endured the challenges of self-discovery, transformation, and solitude, these flames now meet not from a place of need but from mutual recognition, reverence, and a deep understanding of their inner strength. Before these flames can come together, they must go through the journey of individuation, the process of becoming whole within themselves.

Each flame has travelled through the solitude of self-reflection, enduring the sometimes lonely but necessary path of inner growth. They have faced their shadows, embraced their light, and cultivated the wisdom of navigating life's challenges. Both flames have learned the power of being whole and independent in this phase. They are not seeking external validation from others or relying on someone else to complete them. Each flame knows its worth and stands firmly grounded in its purpose, free from the desire to chase after fleeting sources of external approval. They have endured the loneliness that often accompanies personal transformation, knowing that this period of solitude is essential for them to shine fully in their light.

The relationship between these two flames is safe and grounded because it is built on the solid foundation of individual inner strength. Each flame is aware of its light and the beauty it radiates. They are not drawn to one another out of need but out of a deep, shared recognition of the power of their individual and collective growth.

In a relationship where both individuals have done the work of inner transformation, there is no room for co-dependency, manipulation, or unhealthy attachments. There is no need for validation from the other, no need to chase after external approval, or to seek to fill any perceived gaps in themselves. They are already whole, and their union expresses their shared journey rather than an attempt to complete what was once missing. This relationship is rooted in mutual respect and appreciation for each other's journey. The bond they share reflects their individual work, and true intimacy can flourish in this space of inner knowing and self-reliance. There is a deep sense of trust that neither person seeks to control, change, or limit the other. Instead, they are free to be authentic, knowing the other will hold space for their growth and evolution.

In this union, the two flames dance together, bringing their unique energy and light to the relationship. There is no competition, no desire to outshine the other. Instead, they celebrate each other's brilliance and individuality, knowing that their combined energy creates a power more significant than the sum of its parts.

Just as two flames, side by side, burn brighter than one alone, the union of these two souls magnifies the beauty and strength of each other. Their relationship becomes a sacred space where both can continue evolving, learning, and growing together while remaining true to their journeys. The flames do not need to consume each other to burn brightly; they fuel each other's light, creating a harmonious, radiant whole.

A relationship between two flames who have done the work is rooted in a deep sense of purpose and love. They do not seek to possess one another but honour each other's unique path and growth. Their love is unconditional and grounded in mutual understanding, respect, and a shared vision of the future.

In such a relationship, both individuals have reached a point of spiritual maturity where they understand that love is not about seeking to fix the other but about holding space for each other's journey. There is no judgment, need for control or fear of abandonment. Both flames have learned that their worth is not determined by their relationship but by their inner connection to their higher selves. The beauty of this type of relationship is that it is rooted in the truth that both individuals are enough as they are. They are already complete and whole, and their union expresses the love and light they each bring to the world. Together, they create a sacred partnership that allows both to grow, evolve, and shine in their full brilliance.

The final spiritual evolution is the coming together of two flames that have both done the work, endured the transformation, and now meet each other from a place of strength and authenticity. It is a union of equals, two souls grounded in their light and learned to stand in their truth. This union is not a merging of identities or a need for external validation; it is the recognition of each other's unique brilliance and the shared commitment to walk together in love, purpose, and alignment with the divine.

In this sacred union, both flames burn brightly, side by side, each fully expressing their individuality while supporting the other's growth. Their relationship reflects the love and respect they have cultivated within themselves. It serves as a beacon of light to others on their journeys of self-discovery and spiritual evolution or growth. The final spiritual evolution recognises that when two flames come together, their combined energy creates something far more significant than they could achieve alone. Their love is not a need but a choice, an intentional and sacred partnership that amplifies their light and creates a space where both can continue to evolve in harmony and unity.

Visual Task: The Moth and The Flame – A Journey of Self-Reflection

This exercise encourages deep self-reflection. It uses the moth and flame imagery to explore the dynamic between external pursuit and inner purpose.

Step 1: Find a Quiet Space

Begin by sitting comfortably in a peaceful location where you can close your eyes without distractions. Take a few deep breaths, grounding yourself and letting go of the noise around you. This space is for stillness and reflection.

Step 2: Reflect on the Moth

Visualise a moth, restless, unsteady, and constantly in motion. See it flitting from one light source to another, never settling, always reaching outward. Its wings are tired, its path aimless, driven by a need for external validation, chasing wealth, beauty, fame, or relationships.

Ask yourself:

- Am I currently chasing something outside of myself?
- Am I caught up in the pursuit of approval or material success?

- Do I constantly stretch, reaching for things or people that may not align with my true self?
- What distractions make me feel ungrounded, like flying from one flame to another?

Step 3: Reflect on the Flame

Now, shift your attention to the image of a bright, steady flame. It burns with an inner strength that is unwavering and calm. This flame does not chase; it simply exists, radiating light and warmth. It knows its purpose and sacred path, shining fiercely without recognition or external validation.

Ask yourself:

- Am I centred in my purpose, and grounded in who I truly am?
- Do I remain faithful to my values, not swayed by fleeting desires or distractions?
- Am I allowing the universe to guide me rather than striving endlessly for things that may not nourish my soul?
- What is the essence of my inner light, and how can I bring it into the world without chasing anything outside myself?

Step 4: Visualise Your Journey

Close your eyes and reflect on your whole life. Do you identify more with the moth, always seeking, always in motion, always looking outside yourself for meaning, or the intense, centred flame radiating your unique light?

- If you identify with the moth, imagine gently guiding yourself back to balance. See yourself slowing down, returning to your centre, and recognising that your worth is not determined by what you chase but by the light you already carry.

- If you identify with the flame, imagine yourself shining brighter, more fiercely and more clearly. See the world naturally drawn closer to your radiance as you walk your sacred path, aligned with your true purpose.

Step 5: Bring Awareness to Your Path

Slowly open your eyes and take a few deep breaths. Reflect on the insights that arose from this exercise. Ask yourself:

- What steps can I take today to shift from being a moth to being a flame?
- How can I realign with my purpose and step into the full power of my light?

Step 6: Action Steps

Journal your reflections, noting any distractions or sources of external validation you may seek. Write down what your flame, your true purpose, feels like.

- What is the next step on your sacred path?
- How can you move forward in alignment with your inner light?

This visual task reminds us that we have the power to choose. Will we continue chasing fleeting flames, or will we step into the fullness of our light, allowing the world to be drawn to us in alignment with our most profound truth?

Affirmation:

I am the flame, strong and centred.

I release the need to chase after external validation or fleeting distractions.

I trust in my inner light, knowing that I am already whole and complete.

I am grounded in my purpose, unwavering and aligned with the most profound truth of my soul.

I no longer seek approval, wealth, beauty, or fame, for I know that these are not the sources of my worth.

I shine brightly and unapologetically, radiating my true essence into the world.

The universe guides me along my sacred path.

I trust that signs and synchronicities unfold before me, revealing my next steps.

I courageously embrace my purpose, knowing I am here to burn with fierce authenticity.

I am a beacon of light, unbothered by distractions.

As I stay rooted in my truth, I draw those who resonate with my energy to me.

I am not a moth, endlessly chasing. I am the flame, radiant and eternal.

I trust in my soul's journey,

And with each passing moment, I become more aligned with my higher self.

I am the flame. I am whole. I am enough.

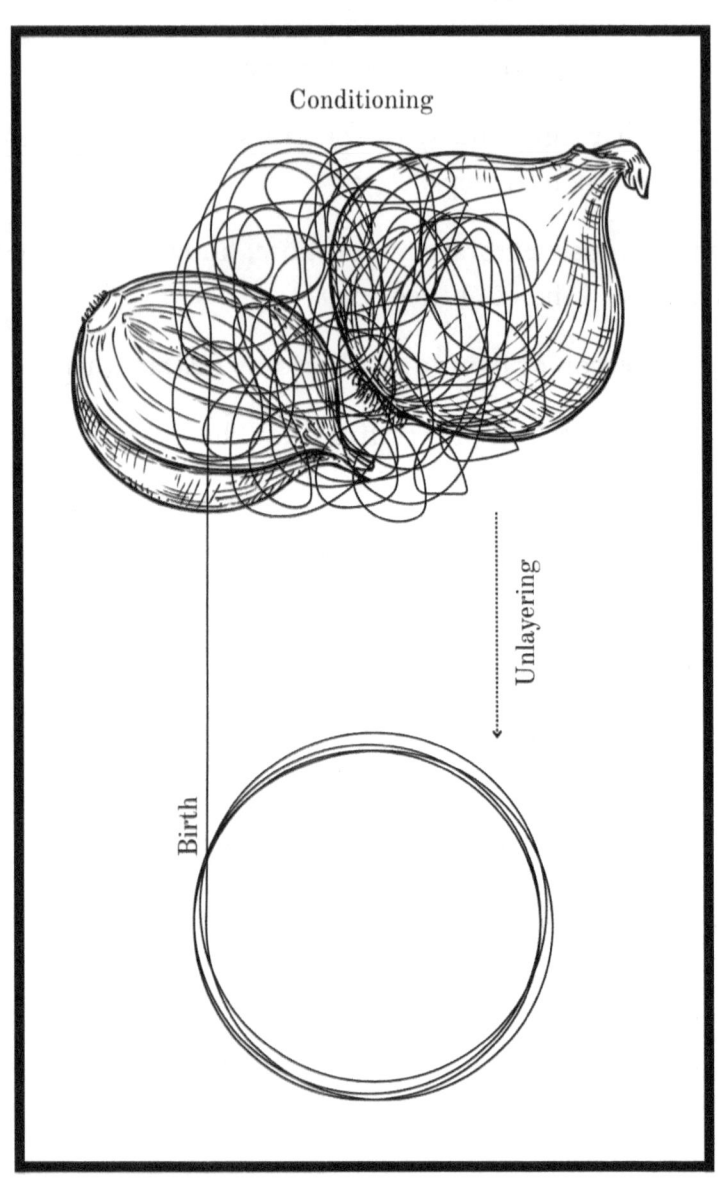

CHAPTER 6
UNRAVELLING THE ONION

"Life starts when one realises that growth is about removing layers rather than adding." - KC Palmer

LIFE'S PATH IS often seen as a journey of becoming. We spend years accumulating experiences, relationships, and achievements, shaping ourselves according to external influences, societal expectations, and family conditioning. Yet, beneath these layers lies our raw, authentic self, untouched, untainted, and pure. Reconnecting with this true self is not about adding more but about peeling away the layers we have accumulated throughout our lives.

The human experience is a delicate process of self-discovery and unravelling, much like peeling back the layers of an onion. Each layer represents an aspect of our conditioning, ideas about who we should be, what we should achieve, and how we should behave. However, in truth, the purest form of being is not found in adding more layers but in removing the layers that obscure our authentic selves.

This chapter explores how human conditioning, through the influence of family, society, trauma, and personal experience, shapes the layers we wear and how, through healing processes, we can begin to unravel them. At the core of this unravelling is the concept of the *shadow self*, those parts of ourselves that we cannot see, the hidden aspects of our psyche that influence our behaviours and thoughts in subtle yet powerful ways.

These shadow aspects often arise from early trauma, attachment wounds, and the unconscious programming we receive as children. Through practices like self-reflection, meditation, or plant medicine, we can start to see these hidden parts of ourselves and begin the process of healing and reintegration. The journey to wholeness requires confronting these shadow aspects, accepting them, and finding peace in the balance between light and dark, masculine and feminine.

The Layers of Conditioning: Early Childhood and Family Influences

Our journey begins at birth when we enter a world ready to shape us. The first forces that add layers to our identity are those closest to us: our parents, family, and caregivers. In these early years, we are like sponges, absorbing everything around us without the capacity for discernment. We internalise the messages we receive from our family members, whether overt or subtle, and they form the foundation of our beliefs about ourselves and the world.

For example, if a child is repeatedly told that their thoughts or emotions are invalid or dismissed, they may grow up learning to suppress their truth. Perhaps you were a child whose creativity was stifled, not because of malice but because your parents did not understand the value of nurturing creative expression. Or maybe they over-loved you, based on their own upbringing and kept you between strict safety boundaries, which denied your expression. This suppression created a layer of self-doubt that may persist into adulthood. As an adult, you may struggle to express yourself freely, constantly questioning whether your ideas or desires are valid.

This early trauma, often overlooked, can become a deeply ingrained pattern that shapes your behaviour without you even realising it.

Similarly, children who grow up with emotionally unavailable or critical parents often develop a deep-seated belief in their unworthiness. Perhaps your family members or friends judged you with insincere remarks or subtle criticism, planting seeds of shame, self-judgment, and self-criticism that you carry with you throughout life. You may have internalised these judgments, unconsciously believing that you are not enough, that your worth is conditional, and that you must seek validation from others to feel whole.

These early experiences form the first layers of conditioning that shape how we view ourselves and interact with the world. They create a mental framework for defining ourselves, relating to others and navigating life's challenges. But, as we continue our journey, we accumulate more layers from external influences, such as school, peers, and society, all of which continue to mould our identity.

The Shadow Self: The Unseen Forces Within

While much of our conditioning is visible and conscious, a hidden aspect of ourselves also profoundly influences us. This secret part of our psyche is often called the *shadow self*. The shadow consists of the unconscious, repressed, or denied parts of ourselves, traits, emotions, and desires we have learned to suppress because they are deemed unacceptable, unlovable, or unsafe to express.

Carl Jung, a Swiss psychologist and psychiatrist who founded analytic psychology, introduced the concept of the shadow, who believed that our shadow self holds the key to much of our unresolved emotional pain and personal growth. The shadow is not inherently harmful, but it contains all the parts of ourselves that we have disowned or rejected. It is the aspect of us that we cannot see, yet it drives much of our behaviour. These unseen forces shape how we react to situations, form relationships and engage with the world, often without conscious awareness.

The shadow self is usually formed in childhood when we are taught which parts of ourselves are acceptable and which are not. For example, if a child grows up in a household where emotional expression is not allowed, perhaps because their parents were emotionally distant or unable to handle their feelings, they may repress their emotions. This creates a layer of conditioning around emotional suppression that forms the shadow. As an adult, this person may struggle with emotional expression and may be unable to connect with or understand their emotions.

The suppressed emotions, however, will inevitably surface, often in unhealthy ways, such as through anxiety, depression, or relational struggles. Trauma, whether emotional, physical, or psychological, also plays a significant role in forming the shadow. Traumatic experiences, particularly those that occur in childhood, create deep scars in the psyche. When left unhealed, these wounds become part of the shadow self and influence how we perceive the world.

A person who has experienced abandonment or neglect may carry a fear of rejection throughout their life. This fear, deeply rooted in the unconscious, drives their behaviour in relationships, often leading them to overcompensate or withdraw when they feel threatened. Trauma, particularly when experienced in childhood, can leave deep imprints on our nervous system. The fight-or-flight response, governed by the sympathetic nervous system, activates in response to perceived danger.

Children who experience traumatic events, whether through abuse, neglect, or emotional instability, learn to be hypervigilant and constantly on alert for threats. This trauma response becomes deeply ingrained in their psyche, influencing their behaviour long after the trauma has passed. As adults, they may react to seemingly benign situations with excessive anxiety, defensiveness, or anger simply because their nervous system is still conditioned to view the world as a dangerous place.

Now, couple early childhood trauma with a job that requires hypervigilance, such as in the military, for first responders, and in high-intensity safety roles, and you have a one-way ticket to a chronically overactivated parasympathetic system. Now add dysfunctional relationships, alcohol or addictions. You can see how the layers of the onion pile on.

The parasympathetic nervous system, which governs rest, relaxation, and emotional regulation, can be overwhelmed by the chronic activation of the fight-or-flight response. Healing from trauma involves retraining the nervous system to shift from a state of chronic stress to one of balance and relaxation. This process is deeply tied to the unravelling of conditioning, the removal of the layers formed because of early experiences, trauma, and emotional wounds. Healing the shadow is a crucial aspect of returning to our true selves.

However, the shadow cannot be healed through avoidance or denial. Instead, it requires integration, acknowledging the repressed aspects of ourselves and bringing them into the light. This is no easy work and may require professional guidance and integration. Psychologists, in particular ones who specialise in Internal Family Systems (IFS), cranial sacral therapies, acupuncture, eastern herbs, meditation, yoga, breathwork, and plant medicine, can serve as tools for this process, allowing us to calm the parasympathetic nervous system and to help confront the hidden parts of ourselves and begin the journey of self-healing.

To break the cycle, one must understand oneself.

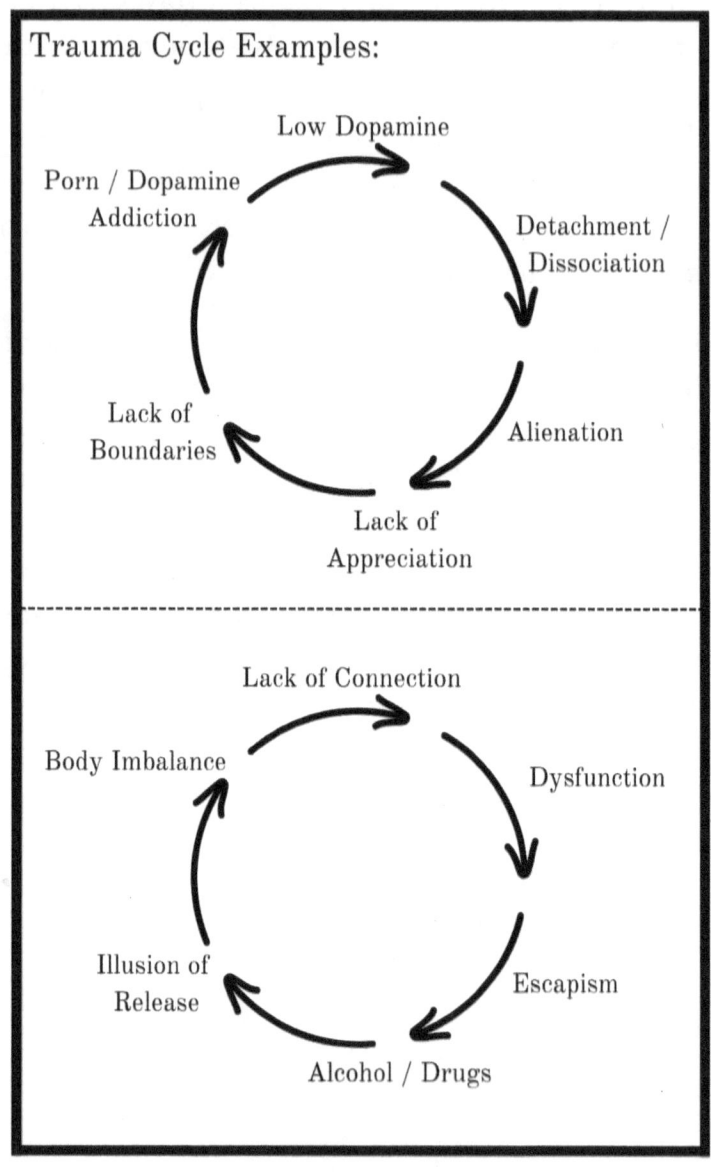

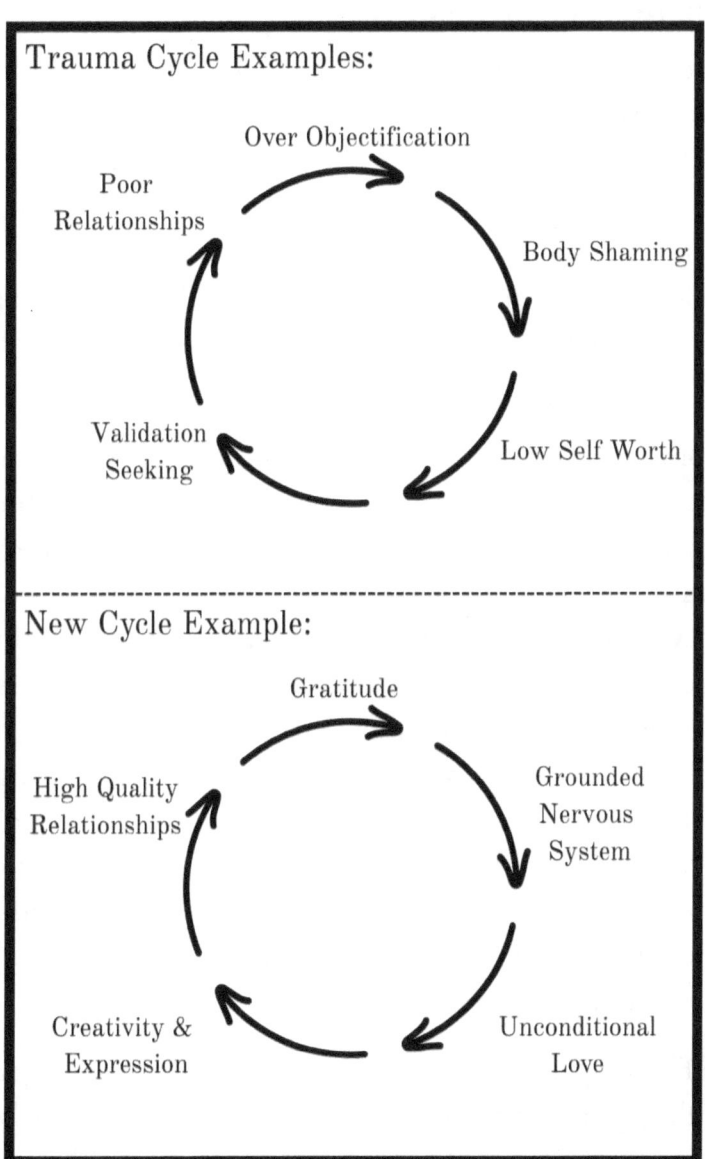

Balancing the Masculine and Feminine: The Journey to Wholeness

Another critical aspect of human conditioning involves the balance of the masculine and feminine energies within us. These energies are not gender-specific but are archetypal forces that exist in all individuals. The masculine energy is often associated with action, structure, logic, and outward expression, while the feminine energy is associated with receptivity, intuition, creativity, and inward reflection.

From early childhood, we are conditioned to embrace one energy over another, depending on our upbringing and societal expectations. Perhaps you grew up in a household where your father was absent or emotionally unavailable, leaving you without a transparent masculine role model. In response, you may have unconsciously adopted a more masculine stance, compensating for lacking a solid foundation in your masculine energy. Alternatively, perhaps your father was highly dominant in his masculinity, and you struggled to express your softer, more feminine side. This imbalance can lead to internal conflict, where one energy is overactive while the other is suppressed.

Self-healing and returning to our authentic selves require finding peace between these energies. As we shed the layers of conditioning that have forced us into rigid gender roles or societal expectations, we begin to understand that both masculine and feminine energies are necessary for our wholeness. The beauty of balance lies in integrating both forces within us, creating a harmonious dance between action and receptivity, logic and intuition, strength and vulnerability.

The lotus flower, often used as a symbol of spiritual awakening, cannot survive without the mud in which it grows. This metaphor highlights the importance of embracing the mud and the lotus: the darkness, the light, Yin and Yang, the challenges and the beauty. In the same way, our journey towards wholeness requires us to embrace the mud of our past, our pain, trauma, conditioning, and shadow self, to fully bloom into our authentic selves. The lotus does not resist the mud; it grows through it, finding its strength and beauty through overcoming adversity. This balance between the light and dark, the masculine and feminine, is the key to integrating all aspects of our being, allowing us to stand firmly in our true power.

The Healing Journey: Embracing the Mud and the Lotus

When we begin the process of self-discovery and healing, we must understand that the mud and the lotus are necessary for our growth. Just as the lotus cannot bloom without the mud, we cannot fully realise our potential without integrating our shadows, traumas, and conditioning. The mud represents all the experiences and layers that have shaped us, both positive and negative. It represents the wounds we carry, the patterns we unconsciously follow, and our limiting beliefs.

It is from this place of deep discomfort and dissonance that we can begin the process of integration and growth. However, the path to healing is not linear. It is not about eliminating the shadow or eradicating pain but about transforming our relationship to these aspects of ourselves. Instead of denying or repressing our shadow, we are called to embrace it and recognise that it is an integral part of who we are. The shadows are not bad parts of ourselves; they are merely aspects of us buried due to fear, shame, or trauma. When we acknowledge them, we invite healing and integration.

Through deep, conscious breathing, we can access the subconscious layers of our mind and release stored emotions, memories, and traumas that may be influencing our present reality. By breathing deeply and consciously, we can shift from a state of fear or anxiety to one of clarity and openness.

Some choose plant medicine to assist in this process, particularly substances like Ayahuasca, Psilocybin, Peyote or Toad (5-MeO), which have been used for centuries by indigenous cultures to access the subconscious and explore the hidden parts of the self. These sacred medicines open a doorway to the unconscious, allowing us to confront the shadows we may have buried deep within us. Through guided ceremonies, it is thought that individuals may experience profound healing, uncovering repressed memories, unresolved trauma, and hidden emotional wounds. Though intense and often uncomfortable, the plant medicine journey integrates the shadow self into our conscious awareness, facilitating a deeper understanding of who we are.

Ultimately, these practices aim to bring us back into balance, into alignment with our true selves. When we begin to remove the layers of conditioning and trauma that have shaped our sense of self, we start to reconnect with the raw, untainted essence that is always within us. This is the true self, the part of us not influenced by external validation, societal expectations, or familial conditioning. It is the part of us that is whole, complete and at peace with itself. These are all vessels to a deeper consciousness. How you reach your path is entirely up to the captain.

The Ocean of Consciousness: Surrendering to the Waves

Consciousness resembles an immense, profound, and perpetually changing ocean. It extends beyond our visual reach, encompassing both serenity and chaos within its depths. To truly navigate this ocean, one must first traverse the unyielding battleground where the waves collide with the shore, the realm of the ego.

The shoreline is where our true selves are revealed. The waves crash against the sand, exposing the false identities, fears, and harmful patterns we hold onto. This is a moment of surrender, where we must allow the tides to mould us, smoothing our rough edges and wearing away what no longer serves us. Here, many individuals retreat, fearing the revelations the ocean might unveil once their facade is stripped away.

However, for those who endure, a more profound journey begins. Beyond this threshold, the sea is not solely serene and placid. The next challenge is interpreting the waves, life's unpredictable, chaotic forces. Some waves are gentle swells that guide us effortlessly onward, while others surge like formidable walls, threatening to engulf us. To navigate this realm, one must cultivate awareness of the waves, the rhythm beneath them and the hidden currents that influence their movement.

Once we establish a foundation of understanding, we learn to move with the ocean instead of against it. In that moment, we stand, riding the waves, not as their controllers but as modest participants in their flowing dance. The ocean is not ours to dominate, only to harmonise with. Every shift and adjustment becomes a conversation between us and the wave, a dialogue of surrender and response.

For a fleeting moment, stillness exists, a perfect equilibrium of motion and acceptance. But the ocean continues, as does life. A fresh set of waves will always appear on the horizon, presenting new challenges and deeper insights. Yet, having stood once, we no longer dread the fall. We understand now that the ocean does not aim to drown us, it teaches us how to ride.

The Path of Integration and Rebirth

As we begin to unravel the layers of conditioning, trauma and societal expectations, we enter a process of integration and rebirth. We are not becoming someone new; we are simply returning to who we always were, whole, pure, and aligned with our highest truth. This is not an easy process. It requires courage, self-compassion, and patience. It requires a willingness to face the parts of ourselves that we have long avoided and confront the shadows lurking in our psyche.

But it is only by embracing these parts of ourselves that we can experience true healing. As we integrate these aspects of ourselves, we align with our true essence. We no longer need external validation or approval because we know we are whole, just as we are. We are no longer defined by the roles, labels, or identities imposed upon us. We are free to be our authentic selves, walking the path uniquely ours with courage, grace, and confidence.

This is the journey of self-discovery, the unravelling of the onion. It is the journey of peeling back the layers of conditioning, trauma, and societal expectations to reveal our true identity. And in this process, we find that the lotus cannot bloom without the mud. The mud is not something to be avoided; it is the soil where the lotus grows. The balance between the masculine and feminine, the light and the shadow, is the key to finding peace within ourselves and creating a life fully aligned with our highest purpose.

X marks the…

Through the fog,
The heavy winds,
You see a light that shines within,
The storm comes,
The sails blow,
For where it goes,
You do not know.
-KC Palmer

Practical Task 1: Breaking the Cycle

Do you remember the timeline exercise you completed when you started this book? It is now time to go back and reflect on your life's cycles. Grab a pen and notebook, create your cycles, and reflect on your habitual behaviours with absolute truth and honesty.

Step 1: Identifying Your Patterns

Observe Your Reactions: Pay close attention to your emotional reactions in different situations over the next week. When you feel triggered, pause and ask yourself:

- What emotion am I feeling?
- What thought immediately follows this emotion?
- How do I typically react when I feel this way?

Trace It Back: Identify patterns by reflecting on these moments:

- What situations consistently trigger you?
- Are there recurring thoughts or beliefs beneath your reactions (e.g., "I'm not good enough," or "People always leave.")?
- Can you connect these feelings to experiences from your past?

Step 2: Mapping Your Trauma Cycle

Visualise the Cycle: Draw a circle and describe the repeating cycle. Use these prompts:

- What triggers the cycle?
- What emotional response arises?
- What thoughts follow?
- What behaviours do you engage in as a result?
- What outcome or consequence reinforces the cycle?

Interconnection Check: Reflect on how your cycles fuel each other. For example:

- Does a fear of rejection lead you to isolate yourself, reinforcing feelings of loneliness?
- How does one emotional reaction create a domino effect on other areas of your life?

Step 3: Designing a New Cycle

Clarify What You Want: Imagine breaking free from old patterns. Ask yourself:

- What kind of thoughts and emotions would I like to experience instead?
- What actions align with the person I want to become?

- What outcomes would reinforce a healthier cycle?
- Create Your New Cycle: Draw a new circle. Define new responses for each stage:
- Trigger: What situations will you face differently?
- Emotion: What emotion do you want to nurture in those moments?
- Thoughts: What empowering thoughts will replace old narratives?
- Behaviours: What conscious actions align with your desired self?
- Outcome: What positive results will this new cycle create?

Step 4: Implement & Reflect

Test & Adapt: Practice responding through your new cycle for the next month. When old triggers arise, pause and intentionally choose your new pattern.

Journaling Practice: Reflect weekly on:

- What triggers did I encounter?
- How did I respond differently?
- What changes am I noticing in my emotions and outcomes?

Affirmation:

I peel back the layers of conditioning, one by one, like an onion, revealing the raw truth of who I am.

With every layer shed, I release old patterns, outdated beliefs, and fears that are not mine to carry.

I break the cycles that no longer serve me, choosing growth over comfort, truth over illusion.

I embrace the discomfort of transformation, knowing that within it lies my liberation.

I am not defined by my past or the expectations placed upon me. I am free, limitless, and ever-evolving.

I stand in my authenticity, grounded in my power, unapologetically myself.

With love and courage, I walk the path of my highest self, fully aligned, fully awake, and fully me.

Practical Task 2: Embracing the Mud and the Lotus

This exercise is designed to help you acknowledge the challenging, painful parts of your past (the mud) and the strengths, growth, and radiance you embody now (the lotus). It is a powerful practice of self-reflection and integration, allowing you to see how your struggles and pain have contributed to the beauty and strength you possess today.

Step 1: Set Your Intention

Take a few deep breaths and set the intention to be fully honest with yourself. This is a safe space for self-exploration, so let go of judgment. Allow yourself to observe what arises without censoring it.

Step 2: The Mud (Your Trauma, Mistakes, and Pain)

On the left side of the page, write down everything that represents your mud. This is where you express the struggles, challenges, and harrowing experiences that have shaped you.

Consider including:

- Past trauma (emotional, physical, psychological)
- Mistakes you've made that taught you valuable lessons

- Painful memories or experiences
- Moments when you felt unworthy, unsupported, or lost
- Patterns of behaviour that have been self-sabotaging or unhealthy
- The shadow aspects of yourself you've avoided or hidden from others

Note: Be as honest and open as possible. There's no need to hold back; this is your sacred space to express your raw, unfiltered truth.

Step 3: The Lotus (Your Strengths, Light, and Uniqueness)

On the right side of the page, write down everything that represents your lotus. These aspects of yourself bring you light, joy and radiance.

Consider including:

- Personal strengths and talents
- Moments of personal growth, resilience, or healing
- Acts of kindness, creativity, or compassion
- Relationships or experiences that have supported your well-being
- Qualities that make you unique or special
- Positive affirmations or truths about who you are

- Your dreams, aspirations, and the vision for the life you want to create

Note: Be honest and reflective. Acknowledge even the most minor victories and the beauty that resides within you.

Step 4: Create a Link Between the Mud and the Lotus

Once you've written down your mud and your lotus, take a moment to reflect on the relationship between the two. Notice how your mud has shaped your lotus. For example, did your pain teach you empathy? Did a challenging experience lead to newfound strength or wisdom? Reflect on these:

- How did your struggles contribute to your growth?
- In what ways has your beauty emerged from the soil of your challenges?
- Can you see how the qualities in your lotus were formed through your mud?

Step 5: Acknowledge the Symbiotic Relationship

Pause and recognise that the mud and the lotus are interconnected. Without the mud, there would be no lotus. Without challenges, you would not be the resilient, wise, and compassionate person you are today. These two parts of you are not separate. They are one. The lotus needs the nourishment of the mud to bloom.

Step 6: Express Gratitude

Write a statement of gratitude for both your mud and your lotus. Thank your struggles for the lessons they have taught you and thank your lotus for the light, love, and growth from darkness. Consider gratitude statements such as:

- I am grateful for the pain I've experienced because it has made me stronger and more compassionate.
- I honour my shadows and light, knowing they are essential to my identity.
- I am thankful for my resilience, healing ability, and the light I bring into the world.

Step 7: Reflect on the Ongoing Journey

In this final reflection, write down your intentions or actions moving forward. Perhaps you want to continue healing, release old patterns, or consciously embrace both sides of yourself. Commit to the ongoing process of integration, where you honour both your darkness and your light equally. Consider affirmations like:

- I commit to embracing my light and shadow, knowing they are integral to my journey.

- I will continue to heal and grow, understanding that every challenge is an opportunity for a deeper connection with my true self.

This task is an opportunity for deep self-awareness and healing. By embracing your mud and your lotus, you recognise that the struggles and strengths you have cultivated are integral parts of your journey. The more you embrace this wholeness, the more you empower your ongoing growth.

This exercise is not about erasing or denying the mud; it's about acknowledging and integrating it as part of the whole. The lotus does not grow in isolation, and neither do we. We constantly evolve through our experiences and understand our true selves through the dance of the mud and the lotus. Remember, healing is not about perfection but embracing all aspects of our being, pain, beauty, shadows, and light. Every step in this process is sacred and meaningful; we continue to grow, bloom, and evolve through it.

Affirmation:

I honour both the mud and the lotus within me.

I acknowledge the pain, the trauma, and the challenges that have shaped me, knowing that they have nourished my growth.

I embrace my shadows, mistakes and the lessons they have offered me, understanding that they are not burdens but stepping stones on my path to wholeness.

I also honour my lotus, light, resilience, beauty, and the wisdom I have gained through overcoming.

I recognise the radiance within me, knowing that it blooms from the very soil of my struggles.

I am both the mud and the lotus, a continuous unfolding of growth, learning and becoming.

I see the perfect balance within me, where my masculine and feminine energies coexist harmoniously.

My masculine energy provides strength, direction, and protection, allowing me to stand firm in my truth.

My feminine energy offers intuition, creativity, and receptivity, allowing me to flow and connect with my soul's more profound wisdom.

Together, these energies form a sacred union within me.

The masculine and feminine, like the mud and the lotus, complement and support each other, guiding me toward my highest purpose.

I do not seek validation or approval outside of myself, for I know that I am whole, radiant, and complete as I am.

I trust the natural flow of life, knowing that every challenge is an opportunity for growth and every moment of peace reflects my inner harmony.

With deep gratitude, I honour my journey.

I release judgment and embrace the truth that I am both the mud and the lotus, the light and the shadow.

I walk my path gracefully, embracing the beauty of my continuous evolution.

I am whole. I am balanced. I am at peace.

And so, what you become has always been.

Conscious Feathers
Bad news, however deep,
Forms a silent poison that begins to seep
Your feathers float in the air,
With a heavy breath of despair,
Your soul will light the misty sky,
Those who see behind the eyes.
-KC Palmer

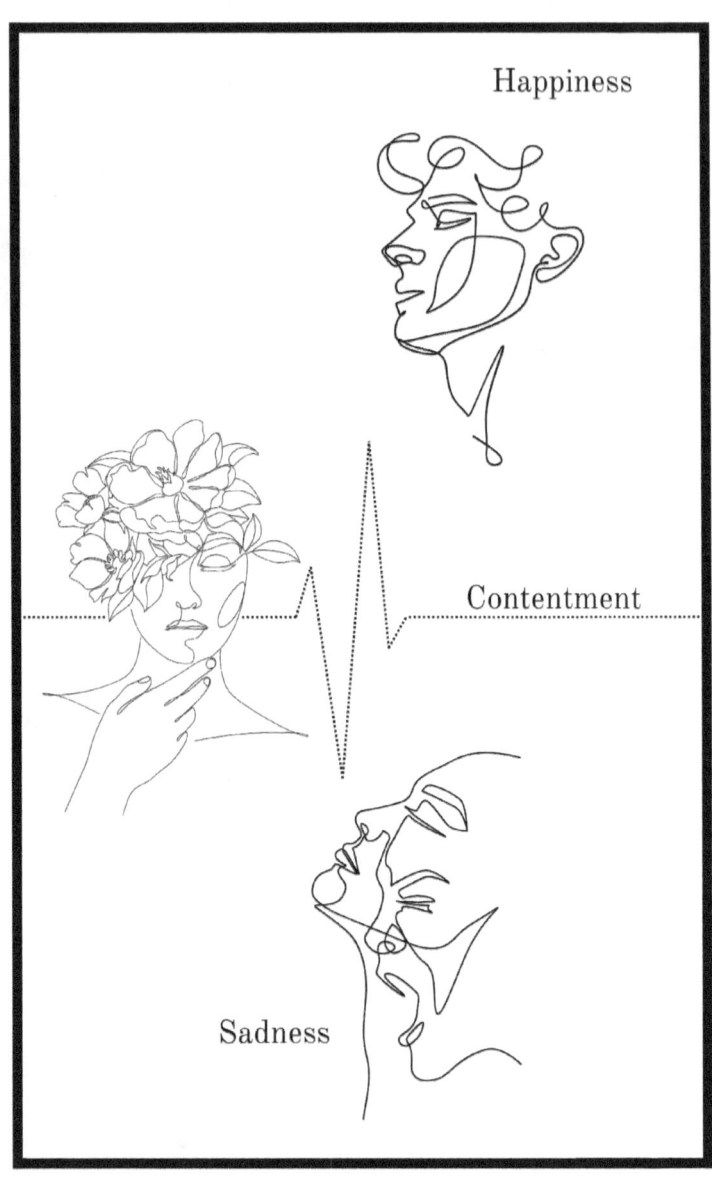

CHAPTER 7
THE ROAD TO TRUE FULFILLMENT

"One is not gifted a flower until one is ready to receive it. To fully nurture means to shine pure sunlight into its centre, to water and endure the winter season when the pretty leaves start to fall." – KC Palmer

The Mirage of Short-Term Happiness

SHORT-TERM HAPPINESS IS seductive. It promises immediate relief, a temporary sense of fulfilment and an escape from discomfort. Whether it's a fleeting sexual encounter, a hit of alcohol, a momentary social validation, or the rush from indulging in other instant pleasures, the feeling often seems like an answer to a deep, unspoken longing. It's like scratching an itch that never seems to go away.

But as satisfying as these quick fixes may seem, they ultimately offer only a surface-level resolution. These experiences bring momentary joy or pleasure, but they fail to address the underlying emptiness that continues to exist beneath the surface. Their effects are fleeting, like a tiny spark that fades when the flame is blown out. The itch returns and the cycle repeats, catching us in an endless loop of craving for more.

Considering the task manager theory discussed in the earlier chapter, what operating system is this attached to? The addiction to these quick pleasures often stems from an unconscious belief that external sources can fill the void within us. Whether through substances, relationships, approval, or even social media likes, we look outside ourselves for validation, for a sense of worth. And though it may give us a glimpse of satisfaction, it never addresses the root cause of our emptiness.

Short-term fulfilment often leads us to grasp quick solutions, making decisions driven by unconscious patterns, habitual reactions, or conditioning. These decisions may seem rational at the time, but they are often impulsive and reactive, based on old conditioning that runs beneath our awareness.

Reflect now on the previous chapter unravelling the onion, and remember that we are built from layers of societal expectations, family dynamics, and early childhood experiences, which form the foundation of how we respond to the world. When we make decisions from a place of unconscious conditioning or lack of self-awareness, we are essentially on autopilot or zombie mode. These decisions are not rooted in conscious awareness but are instead driven by automatic patterns of behaviour and deeply ingrained beliefs.

For example, suppose we grew up in an environment where love and validation were conditional. In that case, we might unconsciously seek external approval through superficial means, such as relationships or social validation, instead of looking inward for true self-worth. These actions are not deliberate or thoughtful; they are a reflex, an immediate response to an emotional need. These unconscious decisions often lead us to repeat past mistakes, causing us to hurt ourselves and others. We become trapped in cycles of temporary relief that offer no real solution to the underlying pain. We may chase after the next high or moment of pleasure, only to find that the emptiness returns once the novelty wears off. In this pursuit, we often make choices that deepen our pain rather than heal it.

The Patient Shade:
Two men walk through the barren desert,
Seeking shelter from the scorching sun,
The first man finds a palm and takes refuge,
Filled with pride, his ego full,
The second marches on, patient and calm,
A few hours pass and he finds a cave,
The first, now burning, he did not account for the movement of the sun,
The second, resting peacefully, today he has won.
-KC Palmer

The Promise of Long-Term Fulfillment

Long-term fulfilment, however, results from a different approach, a patient, methodical and inward journey that allows us to confront the holes in our road and fill them with genuine healing and growth. Rather than masking the pain with temporary fixes, long-term fulfilment requires us to dive deep into the root causes of our discomfort and address them from within.

Imagine a perfect road fully healed and paved with love, care, and understanding. The holes in this road are no longer visible because they have been filled with meaningful, enduring solutions that come from within through personal growth, self-reflection, and inner peace. This path has been gradually built, not through instant gratification, but through hard work, patience, and profound emotional and spiritual healing.

In this process of long-term fulfilment, contentment is no longer a momentary experience. A steady, consistent presence grows over time, like a tree taking root and expanding its branches. This kind of peace comes from aligning with your true self, understanding your inner needs and nurturing your growth in a way that provides sustainable peace and harmony in your life. The road you walk on is no longer full of holes because you have faced the challenges of life head-on, learned from them and filled them with love, wisdom, and understanding.

The End of the Cycle

In contrast to the endless cycle of quick fixes, the path to long-term fulfilment is one of completion. Each step on the journey adds to the stability and beauty of your road until you eventually realise that there are no more holes to fill. The road has been transformed into a smooth, steady path that reflects the peace and fulfilment you have cultivated within yourself. You no longer need to seek external validation or temporary pleasure because you know that everything you need lies within you. You have learned that happiness is not something to be chased but nurtured. It is not an instant thrill but a lasting state of being.

The road may still have twists and turns, but you walk it with grace and confidence, knowing that you are whole, you are enough, and you are on a path that is uniquely your own.

In today's world, happiness has become an elusive goal, constantly sought but rarely attained in a meaningful, lasting way. We are told to chase it, strive for it, and make it the aim of our existence. Yet, in our modern world of constant stimulation, rapid technological advances, and an endless stream of dopamine-inducing distractions, this pursuit of happiness can feel more like an illusion than a tangible reality. It's no wonder many of us feel disconnected from our true selves, grasping at fleeting moments of joy but never truly content with who we are or what we have. Perhaps we should not seek happiness but instead seek something more profound and more grounded, like contentment.

The Paradox of Happiness in a Disconnected World

We live in a time when external sources of stimulation are endless. Technology, social media, constant news cycles, and instant gratification surround our lives. With smartphones in hand, we are perpetually connected to the world, but paradoxically, we are often more disconnected from ourselves than ever. Our attention span has decreased, our ability to focus has dwindled, and the vocabulary used to express our feelings has been reduced to simple words like good or fine.

In a world brimming with rapid-fire stimulation, how can we truly understand what happiness means or even begin to grasp the depth of our own emotional lives? The truth is, as commonly defined today, happiness is often just a high of a fleeting emotion, a rush of dopamine or serotonin released when we get a like on a photo or when we experience an exciting or pleasurable moment. This has never been so prevalent in human history; mass doses of these brain chemicals are released daily, thanks to technology and social media, and our brains are constantly stimulated, sometimes beyond our control.

But here's the catch: these artificial highs are short-lived. They are like a sugar rush that fades quickly, leaving us hungry for more, yet never fully satisfied. We are conditioned to crave these moments of intense joy or pleasure, but the underlying emptiness remains, only to resurface once the dopamine levels drop. We've become so accustomed to these quick bursts of stimulation that we have narrowed our emotional vocabulary to reflect only a small subset of our feelings.

When was the last time you asked someone how they were and they gave you a thoughtful answer? It's rare. Our language has become lazy, and our emotional awareness has been simplified. We've lost the ability to truly express or feel the full range of our emotions. As a result, our sense of self has become fragmented, focused on pursuing highs rather than grounding ourselves in a more profound, more lasting sense of peace.

Happiness has been reduced to a commodity we believe we can obtain through external means, such as material possessions, status, relationships, or from fleeting moments of pleasure. However, these external factors are unreliable and impermanent. As we commonly seek it, happiness is often nothing more than an emotional high, a rush that fades once circumstances change. It depends on the ebb and flow of external events, and as such, it is always subject to the unpredictability of life.

Pursuing happiness, constantly chasing the next high, can become an exhausting cycle. We chase after moments of elation, only to find them short-lived, leading us to seek more and more to fill the void. Each fleeting moment of happiness offers just enough of a taste to keep us hooked, but it is never fulfilling in the long term. It becomes a chase that leaves us tired, frustrated and incomplete. But what if this chase itself is the problem? What if happiness isn't something to be pursued or grasped at all? Instead, what if we could find a deeper, more lasting state of being, one that is grounded in peace, acceptance, and gratitude for everything we already have?

This brings us to the concept of contentment. Contentment is not the same as happiness, though it may often be mistaken for it. Contentment is a state of being at peace with what is. It is a deep gratitude for the present moment and an acceptance of life as it unfolds, with all its ups and downs. Unlike happiness, often tied to intense emotional highs, contentment does not fluctuate with external circumstances. It is a steady, underlying peace that remains constant even when life presents challenges or moments of joy.

When content, neither the good nor the bad defines our experiences. Contentment is rooted in the understanding that you are already whole and do not need to chase anything outside yourself to feel fulfilled. Life may bring moments of joy and sorrow, but you remain balanced, grounded, and centred in each of these. There is no need to grasp happiness or cling to pleasure because you know you are already complete.

Contentment is not passive; it is an active choice to live with acceptance and embrace what life offers without clinging to it. It is about finding peace within yourself so that no external circumstances can shake your sense of self-worth or your internal sense of balance. When you are content, you no longer need to fill the empty spaces in your life with superficial distractions or endless pursuits. You can simply just be.

In our modern world, technology has significantly distorted our relationship with happiness. We live in constant stimulation, bombarded by notifications, images, and distractions. This overstimulation affects our brains in ways previous generations could not have fathomed. Thanks to our smartphones, social media, and instant access to entertainment, the release of dopamine, serotonin, and other pleasure-related chemicals is constant.

While these tools have many benefits, they also diminish the ability to sit in stillness, experience the full range of human emotions, and find peace in the present moment. We have traded our inner lives for external validation, seeking momentary fixes that keep us hooked and dependent on technology rather than developing a deeper, more sustainable form of well-being.

Rather than seeking happiness, the goal is to be content. Contentment is the deep sense of peace and acceptance that arises when we let go of the need to chase after external sources of joy. It is the quiet inner knowing that we are enough as we are and that everything we need is already within us. When we cultivate this sense of contentment, we stop measuring our worth against life's fleeting highs and lows. Instead, we embrace each moment with gratitude for what we have and trust in the unfolding journey.

Ultimately, seeking happiness is like chasing the wind: elusive and always out of reach. But contentment brings lasting peace rooted in acceptance, self-love, and the understanding that we are whole and complete. When we stop grasping at happiness, we open the door to a deeper, more fulfilling state of being, one that is grounded in the quiet, enduring peace of contentment.

Practical Task 1:
Short-Term vs Long-Term Happiness

Divide Your Page into Two Columns.

Label one column Short-Term Happiness and the other Long-Term Happiness.

Step 1: Reflect on Your Current Life

Take a moment to reflect on your current experiences and lifestyle. In the Short-Term Happiness column, write down anything that brings you brief satisfaction or pleasure, those fleeting moments often triggered by external circumstances. These might include:

- Social media likes
- Material purchases
- A quick snack or drink that gives you instant pleasure
- Relationships offering temporary validation or excitement
- Temporary escapes like TV shows, video games, or parties

In the Long-Term Happiness column, write down aspects of your life that contribute to a more profound and lasting sense of fulfilment. These things nurture your soul and well-being over time and might not always provide immediate gratification. Examples include:

- Cultivating meaningful relationships
- Working towards personal growth and learning
- Building a career or passion project that aligns with your core values
- Investing in your health and well-being
- Spiritual practices like meditation, breathwork, or mindfulness

Step 2: Reflect on Your Goals and Desires

Now, shift your focus to what you wish to accomplish in life. Create two more columns: Short-Term Goals and Long-Term Goals. In these columns, write down the immediate goals you're working towards and the larger, more meaningful aspirations that align with your deeper purpose.

For example:

Short-term goals might include:

- Buying a new car or upgrading your house
- Losing weight or improving physical appearance quickly
- Seeking external validation through recognition or awards

Long-term goals could be:

- Creating a legacy or meaningful impact on others

- Building a fulfilling career or lifelong passion
- Cultivating inner peace and emotional resilience
- Strengthening your personal and spiritual growth

Step 3: Analyse the Origins of These Desires

Reflect on the origin of each item you've written in both sections. Ask yourself:

- Is this desire coming from ego? Am I seeking external validation or satisfaction?
- Is this desire from a deeper part of me, my heart and soul, aligning with my authentic purpose?
- Are my short-term desires a way of temporarily filling a void or escaping discomfort, or are they meaningful steps that contribute to my overall growth and contentment?

Step 4: Final Reflection

After completing this task, sit with the awareness of your answers. Notice which desires are genuinely aligned with your more profound sense of purpose and which may be driven by unconscious habits or conditioned beliefs. Acknowledge any patterns or realisations that arise about the nature of your desires.

Practical Task 2: Gratitude Grounding and Reflection

Step 1: Write Down Everything You Are Grateful For

On a clean page, begin by writing down everything you are grateful for in your life. Don't limit yourself to big, obvious things; focus on the small, often overlooked blessings that shape your daily existence. Think about:

- Health, family, friendships, and relationships
- Simple pleasures like a good meal, a beautiful sunset, or a warm home
- Personal qualities like your creativity, resilience, or sense of humour
- Opportunities you've had, lessons you've learned, and moments of peace

Make this list as long as possible.

Step 2: Ground Yourself in Contentment

As you reflect on your list, take a deep breath and sit with the feeling of contentment. Allow yourself to appreciate everything you have at this moment fully. As you do this, ask yourself:

- Do I need anything beyond what I have written here to feel whole, fulfilled, or complete?

- Am I seeking external things, such as status, wealth, or recognition, because I believe they will bring me lasting happiness? Or can I find fulfilment right here, right now, with what I already possess?

Take time to absorb the peace and gratitude that comes from recognising all the blessings in your life. Understand that contentment does not come from acquiring more but from appreciating fully what you already have.

Step 3: Identify Whether Your Gratitude Reflects Short-Term or Long-Term Fulfillment

Review your gratitude list and see if aspects come from short-term gratification (temporary pleasure) or long-term fulfilment (deep, enduring satisfaction). For example:

Short-Term Fulfillment could be things like:

- Getting praise or recognition from others
- Purchasing material goods or indulging in instant pleasures
- Achieving something quickly but without long-term emotional or spiritual depth

Long-Term Fulfillment might include:

- Deep personal relationships built on trust and love

- A meaningful job or passion project that aligns with your values
- Inner peace, health, and emotional balance

Step 4: Reflect on Your Gratitude

Reflect on nurturing the items that bring long-term fulfilment while acknowledging the short-term sources of gratification that may need to be balanced or released for more profound peace.

Final Reflection: The Path of Contentment

After completing both tasks, take a moment to reflect on the path ahead. Consider the balance between short-term desires and long-term fulfilment and the need to cultivate contentment in your life. While short-term pleasures may offer a temporary sense of happiness, they cannot provide lasting peace. True fulfilment comes from grounding yourself in gratitude for what you already have and learning to live with purpose, intention, and balance.

As you move forward, let contentment be your compass, knowing that you are already whole and complete, with all you need within you.

Affirmation:

I am grounded in the present moment and deeply grateful for all I have.

I recognise that true fulfilment lies not in external accomplishments or fleeting pleasures but in the peace I cultivate within.

I honour the balance between short-term desires and long-term growth, knowing that contentment is my true path.

I trust that I am whole and complete and already enough now.

I release the need for validation from the outside world, understanding that my worth is not defined by what I acquire or achieve.

I embrace the beauty of simplicity, finding joy in the quiet spaces of my heart, soul, and life.

I nurture the long-term fulfilment that grows from love, gratitude, and a deep connection to myself and the universe.

I am not in a hurry to chase happiness; instead, I create a peaceful, contented existence rooted in gratitude, acceptance, and trust.

As I move through life, I allow myself to be at peace with what is, knowing that I am enough, just as I am.

I trust in the flow of life and the gentle unfolding of my journey, embracing the harmony between my desires and the present moment.

I am content. I am whole. I am at peace.

And I welcome the light that shines from within, knowing it is all I need to feel fulfilled.

The Glow

Night after night, it begins to raise,
Lonely in the sky, the universe its maze,
Surrounded by darkness close to Mars,
It looks in the distance at the stars,
It ponders life, who am I, who are you,
The mystery remains if only we knew,
Its magnetic pull, the sun its chime,
We can only see you by the reflection of the sunshine.
   - KC Palmer

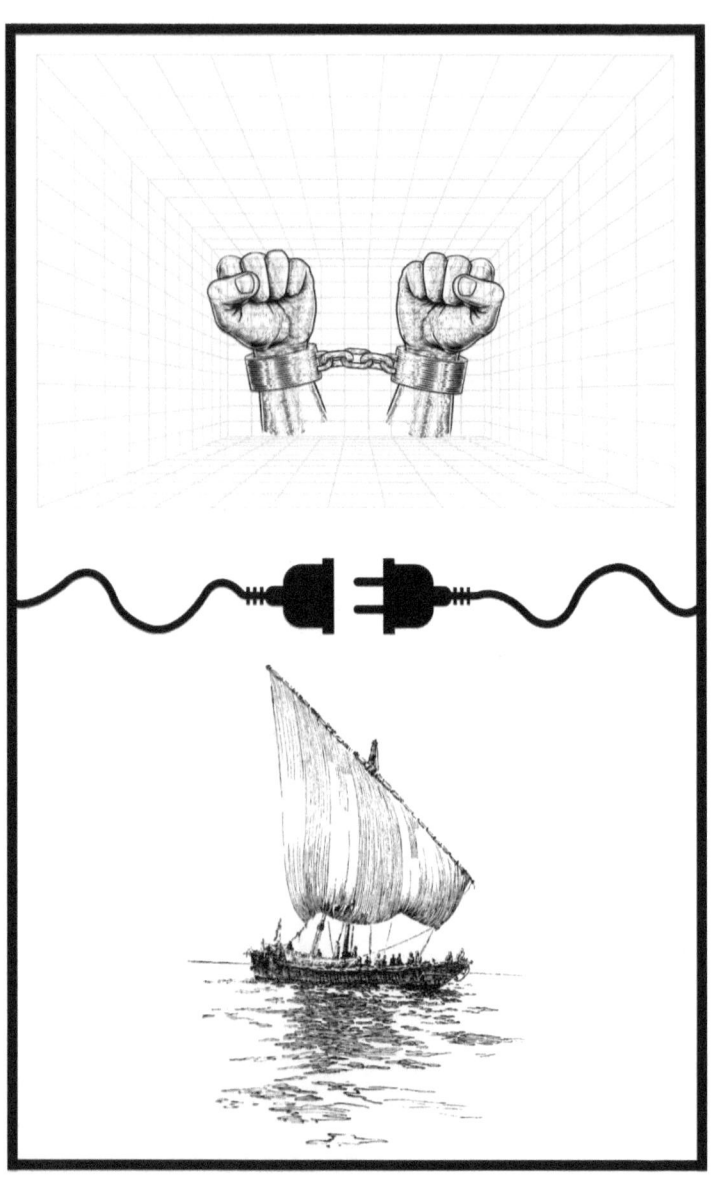

CHAPTER 8
UNPLUGGING FROM THE MACHINE

"Don't cling to what you desire. While expressing gratitude for what you have is essential, avoid becoming too attached. Attach only to what remains unclaimed: the air in your lungs, the sound of the waves, and the rise of the sun and moon. These are constant, eternal, and untouched by time or possession."

IN THE MODERN world, it seems as if technology has taken over every aspect of our lives. From smartphones to the internet, social media and the endless array of consumer goods, we are constantly connected and distracted. Yet, for all the advancements technology has brought us, something profound has been lost: our connection to ourselves, each other and the natural world.

We have become so immersed in the artificial systems of consumption and productivity that we have forgotten our true nature. As we move through life, it becomes increasingly clear that to find fulfilment, meaning, and peace, we must learn to unplug from the matrix of modern life. We must disconnect from the systems designed to distract us and return to our natural, primitive form. This process is not just about rejecting technology or living off the grid; it is about reclaiming our inner autonomy, our innate connection to nature and the ability to think critically and independently.

The Rise of Consumerism and Its Impact on Humanity

At the heart of modern society lies consumerism, a system that drives much of the global economy. Consumerism is the belief that happiness and fulfilment come from accumulating material goods. From a young age, we are conditioned to desire more, to work harder, earn more and spend more. This is the essence of the consumer model: to keep people in a state of perpetual want, always striving to acquire the next thing, the next upgrade, the next best version of themselves, as promised by advertising and marketing.

In many ways, consumerism has led to the creation of a society of distracted individuals. We live in constant anticipation, always waiting for the following product or service that promises happiness. We are bombarded with advertisements everywhere we look, on television, social media, billboards, and even on the devices we carry in our pockets. These advertisements have become so pervasive and persuasive that they unconsciously influence our thoughts and behaviours.

The marketing industry spends billions each year employing psychological and emotional manipulation to sell us products, convincing us that we need them to be happy, successful, or loved. But despite all this consumption, many people feel more disconnected, more isolated and less fulfilled than ever before. We may have the latest cars, the newest clothes and the trendiest gadgets, but we are still searching for something more profound. The constant barrage of consumer messages convinces us that we need more, are not enough as we are, and that fulfilment lies just one purchase away.

This sense of dissatisfaction, this belief that we are incomplete or do not belong, is one of the key reasons why so many people struggle with feelings of depression, anxiety, and loneliness. The more we buy, the more we are told we need and the more we fall into the trap of wanting more. But true contentment is not found in the accumulation of things. It is found in a return to the simplicity of life, where we connect with ourselves, nature, and one another.

The Distraction of Modern Life: Eating, Working, Sleeping

Modern life has turned us into robots, distracted, functioning on autopilot, moving from one task to the next without ever truly engaging with the present moment. We wake up, check our phones, get dressed, go to work, eat, work some more, go home, eat again, and go to bed. Rinse and repeat. This is the cycle of modern life for many individuals: work, eat, sleep and repeat.

The cycle seems endless, offering little time for rest, reflection, or enjoyment. While designed to be productive, this routine does not leave room for deep satisfaction and fulfilment, which is possible when we live in harmony with our true nature. We are so caught up in the demands of the modern world that we forget to stop and reflect, to connect with others, or to nourish ourselves in ways that go beyond the material. Instead of living lives of intentionality and purpose, we are swept up in a tide of obligations and distractions that prevent us from truly thriving.

The idea of working for a living has become so ingrained in our collective psyche that we have forgotten what it feels like to live for the sake of living. We measure success by how much money we make, how many hours we work, and how many products we can afford. But these metrics are hollow. They are not measures of a life well-lived but measures of how well we have been conditioned to function within the systems of industrialisation, consumerism, and capitalism. We live in a world where work has become the focal point of our existence and everything else, including our relationships and well-being, is secondary.

The Overstimulated Monkey: A Frantic Pursuit of More

Despite all their intellect and sophistication, the modern human has evolved into a restless creature that chases fleeting moments of joy or an endless pursuit of growth like an overstimulated monkey grasping at an elusive banana. The overstimulated monkey represents our constant pursuit of more—our relentless drive for success and growth.

We call this progress. We call it ambition. But beneath the polished veneer of self-improvement and material accumulation lies an existence of imbalance that is neither rooted in gratitude nor attuned to the natural rhythm of life. We have traded contentment for conquest and presence for projection. Every moment is spent reaching for what is just out of grasp, convinced that fulfilment is always the next achievement away.

We measure success not by inner peace but by external markers: the job title, the bank account, and the perfectly curated life displayed on digital platforms. Growth is no longer a natural unfolding but an obsession, an addiction to more. We pursue personal evolution as if we were defective in our current state, always needing to be better, sharper, more optimised, never simply *being*.

But what happens when the monkey finally gets the banana? A fleeting burst of dopamine, a momentary rush of satisfaction, quickly drowned out by the realisation that another banana is just beyond reach. And so, the chase begins again.

The modern mind has been trained to seek, not to savour. We do not linger in the moment's joy because we have been conditioned to believe that stillness is stagnation. Enough has become an alien concept in a world where progress is the only acceptable state of being. Yet, nature does not operate in constant acceleration. Rivers flow, but they also pool. Trees grow, but they also shed leaves. The natural world moves in cycles, in a rhythm of effort and rest, expansion and retreat.

But modern humans have severed themselves from this wisdom, believing themselves separate from the forces that created them. Instead of embracing the ebb and flow, they fight against it, resisting the quiet and fearing the pause. True fulfilment does not come from relentless pursuit but from learning to exist in harmony with the present. It is not about rejecting growth but understanding that development is only meaningful when balanced with gratitude. If only we could pause, we would realise that the banana in our hand was enough, that the chase was never the point.

The System's Fear of Free Thinkers

One of the most alarming aspects of modern society is its tendency to suppress free thought and individuality. The system is designed to create consumers, not independent thinkers. Free thinkers challenge the status quo, ask difficult questions, and refuse to accept the narratives imposed on them, threatening the system. Free thinkers are not welcomed within the current system because if people can think for themselves, they will stop being consumers.

When you can analyse the messages you receive critically, the advertisements you are bombarded with and the products being sold to you, you begin to see through the illusion. Stop believing you need the latest gadgets, cars, or fashionable clothing to feel worthy or fulfilled. Instead, you focus on what truly matters: your relationships, personal growth, and connection to the world around you.

The system must keep people distracted to maintain control, so we are constantly chasing the next thing. If everyone were to awaken to the truth of their inherent worth and reject the consumerist mentality, the entire economic model would begin to unravel. They need you to believe you are incomplete without their products and cannot be happy until you have what they sell. This is the lie that keeps the system in power.

The Simplicity of Hunter-Gatherer Life

We must look to the past to understand how far we have strayed from our true nature. For hundreds of thousands of years, human beings lived as hunter-gatherers, dependent on nature for survival. Life was simple yet profound. People didn't need the latest tech gadgets or expensive clothing to feel fulfilled. They only needed the basics: shelter, food, water, and community. In a hunter-gatherer society, survival was a collective effort. People worked together to hunt, gather food, build shelters and care for one another.

The rhythms of nature dictated their lives: the changing seasons, the movement of animals, and the cycles of the moon. There was a deep connection to the land, the environment, and one another. This connection provided the foundation for their well-being, their happiness, and their sense of purpose.

Compare this way of life to the modern world. Today, many of us live in cities, surrounded by concrete and steel, disconnected from the natural world. We live in isolation, working long hours to make money that we spend on things we don't need. We have replaced the communal, tribe-based model with a more individualistic, competitive one. We have been conditioned to believe that we need more than food, shelter, and community to be happy. But the truth is, when we strip away all the distractions, all the excess and all the noise, what we need to be genuinely fulfilled is simple: connection. Connection to the Earth, to each other, and our true selves.

The modern workweek, which dictates the lives of millions of people, is a relatively recent construct. Henry Ford introduced the 40-hour workweek in 1926 as part of the broader industrialisation movement. The idea was to standardise the workweek so that workers would be productive while still having enough time to rest and consume. Ford's system revolutionised labour, allowing workers to spend their hard-earned money on products made by the companies that employed them.

However, the 40-hour workweek is only a century old, and in the context of human history, it is a blink of an eye. For most of our existence, we were hunter-gatherers, living in small tribes and working together to survive. We didn't have the concept of the 40-hour workweek. We didn't have office buildings, computers, or corporations. We had the natural world, community, and the time to live in alignment with the Earth's cycles.

But it is not too late to break free. We can reclaim our freedom by rejecting the notion that we must work within this artificial structure of time and consumption. We can reconnect to the natural rhythms of the world, our ancestors' way of life and the deep sense of fulfilment that comes from living authentically and in balance with nature.

In recent years, there has been a rising movement of people rejecting the traditional path of consumerism and opting for more intentional, conscious ways of living. Many are leaving behind the rat race of corporate life, choosing to work for themselves or to pursue careers that align more closely with their values and passions. They prefer simplicity over excess, authenticity over conformity, and connection over isolation.

This shift is not just a rejection of consumerism but a return to the fundamental principles of human existence. It is about understanding that true happiness does not come from accumulating material goods but from finding fulfilment in the things that truly matter: our relationships, health, and sense of purpose. The modern world has conditioned us to live in disconnection, isolation, and consumption. But it is not too late to reclaim our true nature.

By unplugging from the matrix of technology and consumerism, we can return to our natural, primitive selves, connected to the Earth, each other, and the essence of our being. The path to freedom is not through consumption but conscious living, reconnecting with what truly matters and rediscovering the simplicity and fulfilment that comes from living in harmony with the world.

Task: Unplugging from the Machine and Reflecting on Your Life's Path

Step 1: Find a Quiet Space

To fully engage in this reflection process, find a quiet, comfortable space where you will not be disturbed. Turn off your phone, computer, and any other distractions. Grab a pen, notebook, or journal and allow yourself at least 30 minutes for deep reflection.

Step 2: Reflect on Your Current Life

Start by writing down the answers to the following questions:

- Where are you in your life right now?
- Take a moment to assess your current situation. Write about where you are physically, mentally, emotionally and spiritually. How do you feel about your relationships, career, lifestyle, and personal growth? Are you content? Are you thriving, or are you feeling stuck?
- How did you get here?
- Reflect on the journey that brought you to this moment. What decisions, choices, or events led you to the life you have now? Were these decisions made consciously, or did you follow a path shaped by external forces like family expectations, societal norms, or a desire for status?

Step 3: Why Are You Doing What You Do?

Now, explore the deeper motivations behind your actions:

- What drives you on a day-to-day basis?
- Are you motivated by passion, purpose, and the desire to contribute meaningfully to the world? Or are you primarily driven by external factors like wealth, status, or approval from others? Write about what motivates you to wake up every morning and get to work, whether it's your job, family obligations, creative pursuits, or something else.
- What is the origin of these motivations?
- Dig deeper into the origin of your motivations. Did your desires for wealth or status come from childhood conditioning? Or have you always been drawn to creativity, service to others, or personal growth? Did your family, culture, or society play a role in shaping your motivations? Explore the origins of your desires. Are they authentically yours, or do they have external sources shaping them?

Step 4: Who Are You Benefiting?

This is a crucial question that can reveal whether you're living in alignment with your true self or if you're stuck in the matrix of the system:

- Who benefits from your work, actions, and choices?
- Reflect on the people or systems that benefit from the work you do. Are you contributing to the collective good of humanity, helping others, or advancing a meaningful cause? Or are you supporting a system that values profit over people or simply fulfilling a role that sustains the status quo? Who gets the rewards from your efforts? Is it you, exploitative rich people, or the greater community?
- What role does the system play in your life?
- Reflect on how much of your life is shaped by societal structures, norms, and expectations. How much of your daily existence is driven by consumerism, status-seeking, or keeping up with the pace of modern life? Do you feel free or trapped in a cycle of working to maintain an external image or living up to others' expectations?

Step 5: The Choice for Freedom and Alignment

Finally, ask yourself the most profound question of all:

- Is it time to make a change?
- After reflecting on the answers to the above questions, consider if you are living in alignment with your true self, passions, and authentic

desires. If not, what changes are necessary? What steps can you take to unplug from the system, step out of the matrix and reconnect with your true self? Write down any insights, intentions, or changes you want to make.

- What would a life rooted in passion, purpose, and authenticity look like for you?

- Imagine a life where your actions align with your heart's desires, your choices reflect your actual values, and you are not bound by societal conditioning or the expectations of others. How would your daily life change? How would you feel? What would you do differently? Write down your vision for a life of freedom and authenticity.

After completing the task:

- Take a moment to sit with your reflections. How does it feel to see your life laid out before you? Is there a sense of clarity, relief, or discomfort? Be honest as you assess what is working and what needs to be changed.

- Reflect on your findings and consider whether you can move toward a more conscious, intentional life. Can you slowly begin to unplug from the matrix, the distractions, consumerism, and the patterns of reactivity that keep you stuck? How will you start to align more deeply with your true self and let go of external pressures?

- Return to this exercise periodically to track your progress and see how your thoughts, goals, and motivations evolve. Allow the insights to guide you toward deeper authenticity and freedom.

By engaging in this deep reflection, you take a critical step toward liberating yourself from the unconscious patterns that have shaped your life. This task invites you to explore the possibility of choosing conscious actions, living with intention and creating a life that genuinely reflects who you are at your core. It's a journey of growth and transformation that holds immense potential for your future.

Affirmation:

I am awakening to the truth of who I am. I honour the wisdom within me and trust that my path is authentic and aligned with my soul's deepest desires. I release the expectations and conditioning that have shaped my life and embrace the freedom to live with purpose, passion, and authenticity.

I recognise that the matrix of societal pressures, distractions, or external validation does not bind me. I choose to unplug from the systems that no longer serve me and reconnect with the essence of my being. I trust that my true power lies in my ability to create from a place of love, clarity, and inner peace.

I honour the choices that have brought me here and I forgive myself for any past decisions made in unconsciousness or fear. I now choose to act from a place of balance, grounded in my heart and soul. I can create the life I desire, purpose, joy, and service to the greater good.

I acknowledge that I am part of something far more significant than myself, a universal flow that connects all beings. I trust my journey and know I am becoming more aligned with my truth with every step. I am whole, I am enough, and I am free.

Higher Self

Reflection----Detachment----Positives----Growth

Situation

Reaction----Attachment----Dwelling----Victim

Basic Self

CHAPTER 9
THE DANCE BETWEEN HUMAN REFLECTION AND REACTIVITY

"Change your magnification and zoom out if you are troubled about an emotion, reaction, or event. Zoom out to a bird's-eye view of your life, then go further and zoom out to your country, the world, and space. How can one fixate on such a tiny droplet in a never-ending sea?"

HUMANS ARE NOT just passive receivers of external stimuli; we are highly responsive creatures shaped by our internal landscapes. Conscious and unconscious forces deeply influence how we respond to the world around us, to our experiences, interactions, and challenges. At times, we may react to situations in ways that seem out of proportion or disconnected from the present moment and at other times, we may take the time to reflect, evaluate, and choose our responses mindfully.

These two paths, reactivity and reflection, are both fundamental to human experience. However, in the modern world, many find themselves stuck in a cycle of reactivity, a pattern of social conditioning that can also stem from childhood, trauma, and an overstimulated nervous system. Our relationship with reactivity and reflection is not only influenced by our past. It is also profoundly shaped by the current environment in which we live, particularly by the physical, psychological, and chemical imbalances that can arise from modern lifestyles.

Through an exploration of trauma, the overstimulated nervous system and the impact of stimulants like caffeine, alcohol, and drugs, we can begin to understand the broader implications of how we experience and respond to life. The shift from reactivity to conscious reflection offers us the potential for greater peace, balance, and freedom, yet it requires us to question our habits, our bodies, and how our current world keeps us in tension and imbalance.

The Origins of Reactivity: Flight or Fight Response and Childhood Trauma

Our initial experiences of the world are often characterised by moments of significant vulnerability. As children, we are highly impressionable, and our early life events, particularly those involving trauma or emotional neglect, shape how we perceive and respond to the world for the entirety of our lives. When we face stress, fear, or uncertainty in early childhood, our bodies and minds trigger the fight or flight response, a primal mechanism designed to protect us in times of danger.

Although this stress response is crucial for survival in threatening situations, it becomes less beneficial when it persists as a constant backdrop. Chronic stress, which may stem from trauma, can overstimulate our nervous system, making it harder to achieve balance and calm. The fight or flight response turns into a default mode of operation, even when no immediate threat exists. We cease to react solely to actual dangers, instead being influenced by a deep-seated sense of anxiety or fear that colours our everyday interactions and reactions.

This unconscious reactivity often manifests as irritation, frustration, impatience, and even anger, all exacerbated by our broader environment. Our upbringing, the quality of our relationships, and our experiences with caregivers significantly shape our emotional responses. For example, a child who grows up in an environment where love is conditional or where the emotional needs of the child are neglected may learn to suppress their emotions or develop a deep sense of insecurity.

Over time, these early emotional experiences form the foundation for how we engage with the world later in life. If the child feels unsupported or abandoned, they may develop a heightened sense of alertness, always on edge, ready to react to any slight or perceived danger. This hypervigilance may be carried into adulthood, where it presents itself as an inability to trust, a tendency to jump to conclusions, or an automatic defensive response in times of conflict.

In the modern world, we live in a state of constant stimulation. The fast-paced nature of life, with its incessant demands for productivity, connectivity, and achievement, places immense pressure on our nervous systems. Our attention is pulled in multiple directions, from work emails to social media notifications, advertisements, and news headlines. The brain, wired for survival, responds to this overstimulation with an ever-increasing release of dopamine, the feel-good neurotransmitter associated with rewards. This continuous dopamine rush creates a kind of addiction to stimulation, leading to what can be described as a nervous system burnout. This constant state of alertness impacts our physical bodies.

Stimulants, such as caffeine, are heavily ingrained in our daily routines. Coffee has become a social ritual, a productivity tool, and a means of staying awake. However, caffeine excites the sympathetic nervous system as a stimulant, which controls our fight-or-flight response. Over time, as we consume more coffee and other stimulants, our bodies become desensitised to their effects and our tolerance increases. What once provided a momentary boost of alertness becomes a constant need to keep the nervous system active, preventing the body from ever truly entering a state of calm or rest. This unrelenting pace of modern life can often result in a dependence on stimulants and may lead to an imbalance between the sympathetic and parasympathetic nervous systems.

The Paradox of Self-Help and Chemical Dependency

Despite the overwhelming pressure to keep moving and performing, many people use self-help practices to regain balance. Meditation, yoga, therapy, exercise, and mindfulness are just a few methods people use to restore harmony and clarity in their lives. These practices are essential for cultivating inner peace, reducing stress, and fostering greater self-awareness.

However, there is an inherent paradox in how many of us approach these practices. While we may meditate, read self-help books, and exercise regularly, we often continue to rely on external substances like caffeine, alcohol, and other stimulants to prop us up. This creates a disconnect in our daily practices. We are trying to balance the mind but simultaneously engaging in behaviours that fuel an overstimulated nervous system.

Many people constantly seek stimulation to keep their bodies awake and active while engaging in practices that encourage deep rest and reflection. This dissonance creates a sense of internal imbalance, as the body is in a heightened state of arousal while the mind seeks calmness and peace.

When we continue to consume caffeine or alcohol, our parasympathetic nervous system, which is responsible for relaxation, digestion, and recovery, is inhibited. Both caffeine and alcohol disrupt the delicate balance of neurotransmitters and hormones that regulate mood and energy levels. Caffeine's stimulating effects can lead to anxiety, jitteriness, and difficulty sleeping, while alcohol, although initially relaxing, can disrupt sleep patterns and lead to plummeting bouts of depression or sadness. This constant back-and-forth between stimulation and relaxation, between activity and rest, leaves us exhausted and disconnected from our natural rhythm.

Our unconscious reactions to life's challenges often stem from deep-seated patterns formed in childhood or during times of trauma. Our past experiences, emotional conditioning, and unresolved issues shape these automatic responses to external stimuli. As a result, we may find ourselves reacting to situations with anger, defensiveness, or frustration without fully understanding why.

This is the power of unconscious reactivity: it operates below the surface, dictating our responses without awareness. Unconscious reactivity often leads to negative thought patterns, rumination, and a victim mentality. When we react from this unconsciousness, we may blame others for our unhappiness or feel helpless in our circumstances. This pattern of reactivity perpetuates negative thinking, leading us to feel stuck in a cycle of frustration and resentment.

We may ruminate on past experiences, replaying events, seeking justice or understanding that may never come. In doing so, we become trapped in our emotional narratives, unable to break free from the patterns that continue to hold us back. On the other hand, conscious reflection allows us to step outside the reactive cycle and gain clarity. When we consciously reflect on a situation, we can pause, observe and assess what is happening. Rather than immediately reacting with anger or frustration, we can take a moment to assess the situation, recognise the emotions at play, and explore the more profound lessons or teachings that are present.

This form of reflection leads to greater self-awareness as we learn to detach from the emotional triggers that once controlled us. Conscious reflection is not about denying or suppressing our feelings. Instead, it is about accepting the full range of our emotional experiences, understanding where they come from, and recognising that they do not define us. Through reflection, we can see that every situation and challenge holds a lesson for growth and understanding. By accepting and integrating these lessons, we create space for healing, peace, and freedom.

Reaction Vs Reflection

A reaction is immediate, automatic, and often unconscious. It arises from the depths of our conditioning, past experiences, unresolved emotions, and ingrained patterns. When we react, we're not truly choosing; instead, we let the ghosts of our past dictate our present. This impulsivity is rooted in the primal areas of the brain, particularly the amygdala, which regulates the fight-or-flight response.

Consider a moment of conflict when someone speaks to us harshly. The reactive impulse might be to snap back, escalate tensions, or retreat into defensiveness. Such reactions are mechanical, bypassing the higher faculties of thought and reason. Over time, living reactively breeds chaos both internally and externally. Relationships become strained, clarity is clouded by emotion, and life feels as if it is controlling us rather than the other way around.

The reaction is inherently destructive because it perpetuates cycles of unconscious behaviour. In reacting, we surrender our autonomy to fleeting emotions, allowing anger, fear, or anxiety to govern our conduct. This unconsciousness blinds us to the present moment, trapping us in a feedback loop of pain and misunderstanding.

In contrast, reflection is an act of conscious awareness. It exists in the space between stimulus and response—a space where freedom resides. When we reflect, we step back from the immediacy of our emotions and observe them without identification. This act engages the prefrontal cortex, the brain region responsible for higher-order thinking, rationality, and self-regulation.

Reflection allows us to question our impulses. Is this response aligned with my values? Will it create harmony or harm? Such inquiry disrupts unconscious patterns and opens the door to wisdom. By choosing to reflect, we reclaim agency over our lives and align our actions with intention rather than reactivity. Where reaction binds us to our conditioning, reflection liberates us. It empowers us to respond with clarity, compassion, and purpose. By cultivating reflection, we transform conflict into understanding, impatience into patience, and impulsivity into deliberate action.

The difference between reaction and reflection hinges on the ability to create space, a gap between an external situation and our internal response. This space need not be lengthy; even a few seconds of pause can shift us from unconscious reaction to conscious reflection. Creating space requires practice. In a world driven by speed and constant stimulation, the pause becomes a revolutionary act of reclaiming our attention.

Through intentional practices, we can expand this inner space and develop the capacity to respond with wisdom rather than reflex. Mindfulness practices offer a path to cultivate this spacious awareness. Regular engagement in activities such as meditation, yoga, breath work, and physical exercise trains the mind and body to slow down and observe without immediate judgment. Meditation strengthens our ability to witness thoughts and emotions as passing phenomena rather than absolute truths. Yoga harmonises the body and mind through its union of breath and movement, fostering a sense of inner calm. Breathwork techniques activate and calm the parasympathetic nervous system, allowing us to ground ourselves in moments of heightened emotion. Physical exercise releases stored tension and cultivates discipline and resilience, making us less susceptible to impulsive reactions.

Additionally, journaling provides a reflective outlet to process emotions while spending time in nature reconnects us with a slower, more grounded rhythm of life. Acts of stillness, whether through mindful walking, listening to calming music, or simply sitting in silence, also serve as powerful tools to centre ourselves. These diverse approaches all share a common purpose to deepen our awareness and create the inner space necessary for thoughtful responses. Each practice trains the mind to widen the gap between stimulus and response. Over time, what once provoked an automatic reaction becomes an opportunity for conscious choice.

"Think of everyone as a Buddha; what are they here to teach you?"

Moving Toward Conscious Living

The relationship between human reflection and reactivity is deeply interconnected with our biology, upbringing and environment. The overstimulation of our nervous system, combined with our reliance on stimulants like caffeine, alcohol, and drugs, creates an imbalance that leaves us unable to engage in conscious reflection fully. We often react unconsciously to the world around us, caught in patterns of negative thinking and emotional reactivity that drain our energy and keep us stuck in the past.

To find peace and freedom, we must learn to break free from the cycle of unconscious reactivity. This requires a conscious effort to slow down, reflect, and engage with life from a place of awareness rather than impulse. It also requires an honest examination of our habits, diet, and the external substances that keep us constantly overstimulated.

When we return to balance and nurture body and mind, we can create space for deep reflection, acceptance and ultimately, freedom from the patterns that once controlled us. We cultivate resilience, clarity, and a renewed purpose by embracing stillness and intentional living. In this state of harmony, we no longer react impulsively to stressors but respond with wisdom and self-awareness. True well-being is not just the absence of struggle but the presence of mindful choices that align with our highest selves.

Practical Task: Reflection vs. Reaction

Step 1: Conscious Awareness in the Moment

When a situation arises, whether a conversation, a challenging event, or an unexpected trigger, approach it with pure observation. Here's how you can practice:

Pause and Breathe

As soon as you notice an emotional reaction (e.g., frustration, anger, anxiety), take a deep breath. You don't need to act immediately. Allow yourself a moment to centre yourself. This will help prevent a knee-jerk reaction. Remember, you are not your emotions; you can observe them without being controlled.

Observe the Situation

Become a witness to the event, as though you were watching it unfold from a distance. Ask yourself:

- What is happening?
- What are the facts?
- How is your body reacting? Is your heart racing? Are your muscles tense? Or are you feeling a sudden emotional surge?
- Acknowledge these sensations without judgment.

Ask Yourself:

- How does this situation make me feel?

- Why am I feeling this way?
- What do I need at this moment?

Allow Yourself to Choose Your Response

Know that you can decide how to respond, even if the initial emotions are intense. Do not rush to fix or change anything; allow yourself to fully experience the moment without acting impulsively.

Choose Wisely

From this place of observation, decide how you want to respond. Consider whether a calm, measured response would serve you best or if this is a moment to speak your truth, set a boundary, or express yourself clearly. Choose your next action with wisdom and mindfulness, remembering that you control how you experience and react to life.

Step 2: Reflection After the Situation

Once the situation has passed and you are no longer involved in it, sit down with a pen and notebook to reflect on your experience:

Write About the Situation

- What happened? Describe the situation objectively, avoiding emotional or judgmental language. Focus on the key moments, triggers, and actions.

Explore Your Feelings

- How did it make you feel? Go beyond surface-level emotions and explore why you felt that way. Was there an underlying belief or assumption that led to your emotional reaction? Did past experiences or unresolved wounds contribute to how you responded? Be gentle with yourself during this exploration.

Identify the Lesson

- What is the lesson this situation is teaching you? Did your reaction align with your true self, or did the situation trigger an old pattern or unhealed wound? What can you learn from this? How can this experience help you grow, evolve, or better understand your emotional triggers and needs?

What Can You Change?

- If you need to change your response or approach, write down what you could do differently next time. This is about transforming reactive patterns into conscious, intentional choices. How can you act with more wisdom, peace, and alignment moving forward?

Let Go of What No Longer Serves You

- Ask yourself: What do I need to let go of from this experience? What no longer serves my highest good or growth? Whether it's old patterns, beliefs, expectations, or emotional baggage, release what keeps you from stepping into your most authentic and empowered self. Write these down and acknowledge that you are freeing yourself from them.

Step 3: Integrate the Practice into Your Daily Life

Consistency

- Practice this reflection and response process regularly. It will take time to develop the habit of responding consciously instead of reacting impulsively, but consistent reflection will strengthen your emotional resilience.

Set Intentions

- Each day, set an intention to observe and reflect rather than react. Keep a small notebook with you to jot down reflections as needed. Over time, this practice will become second nature, and you will respond more often from a place of calm and clarity.

Revisit and Reflect

- At the end of each week, revisit your journal and reflect on the experiences you've written about. Assess your progress and growth. Celebrate the moments where you made mindful choices and continue refining areas where you can grow.

Affirmation:

I am the observer of my thoughts, emotions, and reactions. I can choose how I respond to life's experiences in every moment. I trust my ability to pause, breathe, and create space between stimulus and response. I honour the wisdom within me to reflect, learn, and grow from every situation I encounter.

I release the need to react impulsively or from a place of fear. I welcome each challenge as an opportunity to step into my highest self, responding calmly, clearly, and compassionately. I trust that in every moment, I can shift my perspective, see the lesson and choose with intention.

I let go of past patterns and old wounds that no longer serve me. I embrace the freedom to respond consciously, rooted in love, truth, and balance. My reactions are no longer governed by unconscious triggers but by the clarity and wisdom deep within me.

I am grounded in the present moment, at peace with my feelings and free to choose how I experience life. I create my responses and choose peace, understanding, and growth in all I do.

The IBIS

The ancient Egyptians worshipped the Ibis,
A sacred symbol of the god, Thoth,
Whose responsibility was maintaining the universe, judging the dead,
And overseeing systems of magic, writing, and science,
A curious observation when one passes by,
What are your thoughts when observing such a bird?
Where did my judgement originate from?
And now, the dualities of such.
  -KC Palmer

CHAPTER 10
CONNECT TO SOURCE AND INTEGRATION

"We are all sacred mirrors and reflectors. We must pay close attention and carefully observe the types of people who enter our lives. What is being reflected to you?" – KC Palmer

IN THE GRAND tapestry of existence, one thing remains constant, one thread that weaves through the core of our being: connection to Source. Source, God, and the Divine are terms used across cultures, religions, and philosophies to describe the infinite intelligence and creative force that underlies all that is. Connecting to the Source is not just a practice or belief; it is the essence of our existence. The spark of life breathes through us, and it is the guiding force behind our every step. It is the eternal truth that sustains us through every experience.

We live in a world dominated by the physical realm, the visible, the measurable, and the material. We rely on our senses, on our eyes, to navigate the external world. However, as we live in this world, it is crucial to remember that the eyes and the physical aspects of life represent only 10% of our experience. The remaining 90% lies behind our eyes, in the unseen realm, in the realm of the soul and the divine. This is where our true essence resides. This is where our connection to Source exists.

One of the most profound realisations in life is that everything we seek in the external world already exists within us. The answers to our most profound questions, the solutions to our problems, the wisdom we are searching for, all lie dormant within the heart and soul, waiting to be awakened. Yet many spend their lives seeking externally, never realising that we carry the universe within us.

This deep knowing is a part of us, woven into the very fabric of our being, accessible through the simple yet profound act of going within. Many people have known the practice of going within across time and cultures. Meditation, prayer, breathwork, and other sacred modalities are all tools designed to help us reconnect with the divine within. These practices allow us to step beyond the limitations of the mind and the noise of the external world and tap into the infinite wisdom that resides deep within us. By quieting the mind, stilling the body and upgrading our vibrations to the subtle energies of the universe, we can begin to feel the presence of the Source.

It is essential to recognise that the answers we seek in the external world, the approval of others, material wealth, fame, or success, are fleeting distractions. They can never fulfil the deep yearning of the soul to return home to Source. The peace we crave, the clarity we seek and the love we desire are all accessible when we turn inward.

The Witnessing of the Self: From the Unconscious to the Observer

The journey to enlightenment, or spiritual awakening, begins with a shift in consciousness, a movement from unconscious reaction to conscious observation. Humans are often trapped in the whirlwind of their unconscious minds, reacting to external circumstances, thoughts, and emotions. Past experiences, traumas, and societal programming condition these reactions. We live like robots in many ways, following patterns and scripts written by forces outside our conscious awareness.

However, the path to spiritual awakening begins when we step back and become the witness. The witness is the part of us that is separate from the thoughts, emotions, and reactions of the mind. The observer can see the patterns and stories we have created without being attached. This is the first step in reconnecting with Source, to rise above the noise and chaos of the mind and observe our thoughts and actions from a place of neutrality.

When we begin to witness ourselves, we start to realise that we are not our thoughts. We are not our emotions. We are not our past. We are not the roles and identities we have taken on. We are something far more significant. We are the consciousness that observes all these things. The moment we step into the role of the witness, we take the first step toward enlightenment, the first step toward reconnecting with Source.

This process of witnessing allows us to break free from unconscious patterns. When we step back and observe our reactions, we can understand the origins of our thoughts and actions. We begin to see the patterns running our lives, the habits, beliefs, and fears that have kept us from our true nature. As we witness ourselves with love and compassion, we begin to uncover the layers of conditioning that have separated us from our divine essence.

The Unseen Realms: Beyond the Physical

The inner world is a vast and mysterious realm. When we explore it through meditation, prayer, or other spiritual practices, we tap into an infinite source of wisdom and creativity. This is not merely an abstract concept but a real and tangible experience.

Many people who have spent time in deep meditation or prayer can attest to the profound sense of peace, clarity and connection that arises when they go within. In these moments, we feel the presence of Source, the divine energy always with us, guiding and supporting us on our journey. The power of the inner journey is that it connects us to the more extensive web of life. We are not separate from the universe; we are one with it.

Just as a plant is nourished by the soil, water and sun, we are nourished by the divine energy that flows through all creation. When we connect with the Source, we reconnect with the sacred flow that runs through us. This connection brings us a sense of peace, purpose, and alignment. We realise that we are not alone in the world; we are part of something much more significant that transcends time and space.

In the same way that we nurture a plant by providing it with the right environment, we can promote our connection to Source by creating an atmosphere of stillness, love, and acceptance. When we make space for the divine within, we allow ourselves to be guided by the wisdom of the universe rather than the conditioned patterns of the mind.

Within life's grand design, we often view our experiences as threads woven solely into the fabric of our existence. We perceive joyous and painful events as markers of our journey, shaping who we are and what we will become.

But what if the moments that unfold before us are not just for us? What if the universe moves so that our experiences ripple beyond ourselves, influencing the lives of those around us, sometimes in ways we may never fully comprehend?

Consider a simple misfortune: you return from a nature walk only to realise you've lost something valuable along the way. Frustration bubbles up and, in your mind, echoes the familiar lament in your mind: "Why does this always happen to me?" At that moment, it seems the event is meant only for you, to challenge your patience, test your mindfulness, or perhaps teach you the art of letting go.

But as the story unfolds, a greater truth emerges. You decide to return to the trail, and on a whim, you invite a friend to accompany you. You do not yet know that your friend has had an unbearable day, one misfortune after another, compounding into an intolerable weight. They would not have thought to take time for themselves, to step away and breathe in the rhythm of nature. Yet, through the seemingly insignificant loss of your item, they find themselves on a path they would not have otherwise walked.

The breeze calms them, the towering trees remind them of resilience, and in that moment, they reset. You retrieve your lost belongings but gain something more profound, an understanding that this incident was not just for you.

It was an intricate part of something greater, something interconnected. What once felt like an inconvenience was a perfectly placed mechanism of alignment, not only for you but for another soul who needed it more.

Now, imagine extending this perspective to everything that occurs in your life. The missed opportunities, the unexpected delays, the hardships, and even the moments of bliss. What if they are not just shaping you but also playing a role in the lives of those around you? What if your struggles whisper wisdom to someone watching from afar? What if your triumphs spark hope in a stranger? What if the weight you carry today is lightening the burden of another without you even knowing?

Life is not a linear experience lived in isolation; it is a symphony where every note influences the whole. Every experience, whether perceived as fortunate or unfortunate, is an offering to the collective consciousness of humanity. Your suffering is not meaningless, nor is your joy merely your own. It belongs to the vast, interconnected web of existence, where every moment serves a purpose beyond what our individual minds can grasp.

This realisation does not demand blind acceptance or passive surrender but rather an openness to the mystery of how life unfolds. It invites us to release the grip of control and trust that every event, however trivial or profound, is a part of something beyond our singular understanding. It is an invitation to live with a deep and abiding sense of peace, knowing that what happens to us is, in some way, also happening to others.

So, walk forward, not frustrated at what life brings, but with a quiet curiosity. Perhaps the discomfort you feel today is a gift to another. Maybe the detour is not meant to hinder you but to align someone else with their path. And perhaps, just perhaps, every moment is an offering, not just to you but to the entire unfolding of existence itself.

Flow Like a Stream

Do not move at the frantic speed of a thoughtless city-goer, rushing, unaware, and consumed by the ticking of the clock and the weight of material pursuit. A life in relentless haste is not a truly lived life but a series of tasks, a blur of moments passing unnoticed. Yet, do not drag your feet in hopeless inertia, waiting for life to come to you, expecting your dreams to manifest without motion. Stagnation breeds decay, just as water left still becomes lifeless.

Instead, be like the stream, calm, flowing, and steady. It moves with purpose, yet never in haste. It pours gently over the Earth, nourishing the land, shaping the rocks, and bringing life to all it touches. The stream does not force its path, nor does it resist change. It simply moves, adapting to the terrain, yet always finding a way forward.

Imagine your anchor is this flowing stream, your essence, your presence in the now. Your ambitions, your life's path, act as a joining lake, increasing the current, pulling you forward with greater force. Sometimes, the journey leads to a waterfall, a significant drop, an achievement or a failure, or a moment of reckoning. But even as the water crashes below, it does not cease to exist. It regathers, returns to the stream, and continues flowing.

There is wisdom in water. It teaches us to move with life, not against it. We must embrace momentum without force, accept obstacles as part of the path, learn from each twist and turn, and always return to our natural flow. So, flow like the stream. Let life guide you to other currents, lessons and experiences. But always return to yourself, calm, steady, and ever-moving.

The Journey Home: Returning to the Self

The goal of the spiritual journey is to return to our true self, the self that perfectly aligns with the Source. This is the path of awakening and remembering who we are. As we reconnect with the divine within, we realise that we are not separate from the universe; we are the universe. We are the divine experiencing itself through the human form.

When we awaken to this truth, we begin to live from a place of deep knowing and inner peace. We no longer seek fulfilment from external sources because we are already whole. We are not incomplete or lacking; we are full of divine potential. The search for external validation, material success, and fleeting pleasures falls away, and we begin to live in alignment with our higher purpose, the purpose revealed through our connection to the Source.

In many ways, the journey to enlightenment is a journey home, a return to the truth of who we are. It is a process of remembering and reconnecting with our divine energy. As we continue this journey, we begin to experience the profound peace, love, and wisdom that comes from living in alignment with our true nature. And in this space, we are free.

The most important thing to our existence is our connection to the Source. It is the divine energy that flows through us, the wisdom that guides us, and the love that sustains us. By practising meditation, prayer, and other spiritual modalities, we can reconnect with this Source and tap into the infinite potential that lies within us. The answers to our most profound questions, the wisdom we seek, and the peace we yearn for are already within us, waiting to be discovered.

When we step into the role of the witness, we begin to uncover the truth of who we are and take the first steps on our sacred path. This path leads us back home to ourselves, the Source, and the divine truth that has always been within us.

Throughout this exploration, we've discussed the essential themes that can lead to a life of deeper meaning: connection, self-awareness, balance, and inner peace. These principles are abstract ideas and practical tools that can guide us to a simpler, more harmonious life, one rooted in alignment with our true selves and the divine source.

We began by discovering we are all sacred mirrors, attracting and deflecting certain people and energies. We reflected on our inner speed driving on the highway of life and how we can cultivate deeper connections by observing the iceberg beyond the surface. In today's fast-paced world, it's easy to become reactive, driven by unconscious thought patterns, trauma, and overstimulation. However, we can reclaim our power through conscious reflection, mindfulness, and observing rather than reacting.

By stepping into the role of the witness, we break free from unconscious patterns and respond with wisdom and compassion, leading to deeper understanding and detachment from negative cycles. Integrating masculine and feminine energies is another key aspect of balance and wholeness. By honouring the nurturing, intuitive, and creative feminine energy and the strategic and protective masculine energy, we find harmony within ourselves. This balance frees us from seeking external validation because we come to understand that everything we need is already within us. We become the firm, centred and radiant flame and can face life with clarity and purpose.

At the heart of this journey is our connection to Source, whatever we call it. This divine energy is the guiding force of our lives. We can quiet the world's noise through meditation and prayer and reconnect with our essence. When we tap into this connection, we realise that all the answers we seek are already within us. We no longer need to chase external success, possessions, or validation. Instead, we cultivate inner peace, joy and contentment.

This leads us to understand that true fulfilment is not found in the external world but in the simplicity of being. Rather than chasing transient moments of happiness, we learn to embrace contentment in every moment. Life becomes less about the highs and lows of fleeting emotions and more about a steady, peaceful alignment with our true nature. This alignment brings fulfilment, not from external achievements, but from the realisation that we are already whole and complete.

We must care for our physical bodies and environment to live harmoniously with nature and our being. By nourishing our bodies with wholesome food, creating peaceful spaces, and prioritising practices that nurture our well-being, we align ourselves with the natural flow of life. Our body is the vessel for our soul; by caring for it, we strengthen our connection to the divine.

Ultimately, the path to a life of purpose and fulfilment lies in reconnecting with the wisdom within. When we live in alignment with our heart, mind, and soul, we no longer need to seek fulfillment outside of ourselves. True joy comes from embracing the simplicity of life and trusting in the divine guidance always available to us. The universe is ready to guide us; our only task is to listen, trust, and step into our light.

> *"Life is like a pendulum, in order to find your true centre, you have to start swinging"*
>
> - KC Palmer

Practical Task: Deepening Connection to Source and Cultivating Inner Awareness

1. Daily Witnessing Practice

- Set aside 5-10 minutes each morning and evening.
- Sit in a quiet space and focus on your breathing.
- Observe your thoughts as they arise without judgment. Label them as thought, emotion, or sensation.
- Ask yourself, *"Who is observing these thoughts?"* Feel the presence of the witness.

2. Flow Like a Stream – Embodying Fluidity

- Identify one area of your life where you feel stuck or resistant.
- Each day, practice "softening" into that experience. Release mental tension by affirming:
- *"I trust the natural flow of life. I adapt and move with grace."*
- Journal how situations evolve when you embrace flow rather than force.
- 3. Sacred Inner Connection Practice

- Dedicate 10 minutes each day to a spiritual practice of your choice (meditation, prayer, breathwork).
- During this time, ask, *"What wisdom does Source wish to reveal to me today?"*
- Write down any insights, feelings, or intuitive nudges you receive.

4. Expanding the Ripple – Offering Your Light

- Each day, perform one intentional act of kindness (a smile, a message of support, or an offering of wisdom).
- Reflect weekly on how these actions may ripple beyond your awareness.

5. Weekly Integration & Reflection

- Set aside 20 minutes each Sunday to review your journal.
- Reflect on these questions:
  - What patterns or insights emerged from observing my mind?
  - How did embracing flow shift my experience of life?
  - What messages did Source reveal, and how can I embody them?

- How did my conscious actions impact others around me?

Affirmation:

I am eternally connected to the infinite Source of wisdom, love, and creation. Within me lies a wellspring of truth that flows from a place beyond thought, a knowing that transcends the limits of my mind. In each moment, I trust that the guidance I seek is already present, gently revealing itself as I open my heart and quiet my soul.

I am not merely the experiences I encounter nor the emotions I feel. I witness all that unfolds, grounded in a deeper awareness that remains unshaken by life's passing storms.

As I observe myself with compassion, I release the patterns that no longer serve me and allow my truest essence to shine. I am a unique expression of the Divine and a part of the vast, interconnected whole. Every step I take, whether seen or unseen, ripples through existence with purpose and meaning. I embrace the unfolding of my path with trust, knowing that even in moments of uncertainty, I am being guided toward my highest good.

I am here to live fully, to embody love, and to shine light into the world. I align more deeply with my divine essence with every breath, moving with grace, purpose, and unwavering faith.

For all booking enquiries including 1 on 1 or group sessions, speaking engagements, or media requests, please reach out to: consciousenquiry@gmail.com

www.ingramcontent.com/pod-product-compliance
Lightning Source LLC
Chambersburg PA
CBHW020529080526
44583CB00013B/790